# THE SPLENDOUR OF ASIA

# THE SPLENDOUR OF ASIA

## The Story and Teaching of the Buddha

by

**L. ADAMS BECK**

GYAN

*Published by*

GYAN

Gyan Publishing House
5, Ansari Road
Daryaganj, New Delhi-110002
Phone: 011-47034999, 9811692060
E-mail: books@gyanbooks.com

*Distribution Network*
gyanbooks.com
India, USA, Canada, UK, Australia, France



ISBN : 978-81-212-6079-4 (PB)
First Published, 1927

2nd Impression 2021

*Printed at:* Gyan Press, Delhi.



**The Splendour of Asia**
Author: L. Adams Beck

# THE SPLENDOUR OF ASIA

## THE STORY AND TEACHING OF THE BUDDHA

*by*

L. ADAMS BECK

Author of "The Way of Stars," "The Treasure of Ho," etc.

1927

*I dedicate this book to*

ELLERY SEDGWICK

WHO INSPIRED ME WITH THE IDEA

OF WRITING IT

# PREFACE

I HAVE endeavoured in this book to make not only the story but the teaching of the Buddha intelligible and human, so that those who wish to understand one of the greatest facts in history may not find themselves entangled in the mazes of scholastic terms, and may perhaps be enabled to realise its strange coincidences with modern psychology and certain scientific verities. The teaching of the Indian Prince has indeed nothing to dread from science. Sir Edwin Arnold's beautiful *Light of Asia* ends very early in that great ministry, and I have continued the story to the death of the Buddha, and have enriched it with many scriptures and ancient traditions unknown to or unused by Sir Edwin. Words would fail me if I attempted to express how necessary I think a knowledge of this high faith and philosophy is to leaven the materialism of the West, and the reception my books on cognate subjects have had encourages me to think there may be those who will see in what I here set down a great revelation of truth. It is, at all events, a truth which influenced not only the mightiest thinkers of Greece and Rome, but also the beginnings of Christian teaching—which it antedated by five or six hundred years. It may well claim kindred with all the great faiths, persecuting and opposing none which differ with it, and this for reasons which are easily seen in the teachings themselves. In relation to its noble and scientific austerity no words are needed.

Of the Founder himself I may quote a great Buddhist scholar's opinion, one which none who have studied the subject impartially will controvert. "Perhaps never while the world has lasted has there been a personality who has wielded such a tremendous influence over the thinking of humanity. And whoso recognises this will also recognise that almost two and a half millenniums ago the supreme summit of spiritual development was reached, and that at that distant time in the quiet hermit groves along the Ganges already had been thought the highest man can think."

Of the august beauty of the Life those who read will form their own judgment. It has been the mainspring of the highest art of Asia. It has brought peace to myriads. It will bring it to many more.

I have consulted all the available Scriptures, and have not forgotten the great traditions. I am indebted to all the best known scholars, including Max Müller, Faüsboll, Dahlke, Rhys Davids, his accomplished wife, Beal, and many more. I must mention Professor Radhakrishnan and other Indian writers, and among illuminating thinkers I must not forget Dr. Carus, and Mr. Edmond Holmes. To the latter's work I owe a debt because he appears to me to appreciate more keenly than other writers the true point of junction between the early and later interpretations of the Buddha's teaching. I have myself had the advantage of studying later Buddhist interpretation with Japanese scholars, with whom I have translated the Buddhist Psalms of Shinran Shonin. About some of the interpretations there will always be points of difference until we have access to the whole body of ancient teaching in the Far East as well as in India, and freedom from all error is beyond hope.

If any Buddhist scholars should look into this book they will recall the immense difficulty of (so to speak) translating their work for the public, especially where the words of one language often fail to represent the thought of another. They will therefore be lenient to shortcomings. They will note that I have employed Pali or Sanscrit words and names alternatively as I thought they would be more familiar or easier to remember. *Karma* for *kamma*, and *Nirvana* for *Nibbana* are instances of many others. I have omitted accents as mystifying to those unfamiliar with Indian languages.

I can scarcely hope to satisfy scholars and the general public. But if I succeed in interesting some of the latter, the former will, I think, recognise that my aim was justified.

L. Adams Beck.

# CONTENTS

# PART I

## CHAPTER I

THUS have I heard:

Nearly two thousand five hundred years ago, in the City of Kapila in Northern India, the spring came with glory. And surely nowhere in all the three worlds is spring more gracious, for the sunshine, life-giving, inspiring, draws divine scents from moist earth and the deep luxuriance of leaves and flowers to send on every breathing breeze pure incense from the world, rejoicing as a bride in the all-enfolding delight.

Here stood the little City of Kapila, nobly placed, as beseems the birthplace of the Perfect One, and above it the Himalayas stormed the skies with tossing billows of snow, leading the aspiration of man on and up until it melted in the Divine. On these, as was known, the Divinities had their dwelling. Thence Indra, the heavenly lord, drove his flocks of clouds to pasture in pure air, taking form and colour from the splendours of the sun and the moon and the silver embroidery of the constellations. Vaya, lord of the winds, charged in thunder or breathed in music from awful heights of snow. Surya, the Sun, urged his golden steeds from the low horizon to the zenith and on to the confines of night. Chandra, the moon, rose on the crest of the mighty range and sank below it into his mysterious kingdom in the darkening west. The deep pine forests clothing the lower spurs and veiling the sources of the rivers must surely have their indwelling spirits, and the river Rohini, breaking light-foot from the heights to scatter her diamonds as she leaped from rock to rock or brooded a moment in deep pools mirroring her ferns and flowers—what was she but a lovely, living nymph, a Dancer, pure as the silver peaks that fathered her? Therefore let it be known that this city was set among celestial influences, that the gates of the Paradise of India were not far from it, and that the Four Celestial Kings were its wardens. And it dwelt at this time in a great peace.

The city and surrounding country, a part of the great kingdom of Kosala, were inhabited by the Sakya clan. Very great was the kingdom of Kosala. The vast and holy city of Benares, a hundred miles south from Kapila, was but one of its cities, and its capital, Savatthi, lay in the cloudy mountains of Nepal. To the south-east lay the kingdom of Maghada, and only the great Gods then knew to which of these kingdoms would fall the sceptre of India.

And peaceful was the City of Kapila, the City of Red Earth, home of the Sakya clansmen, a race strong and high, for they were of the Arya, the Noble People, and it was they who descending into India through the passes had conquered the dark men of the land and driven them before them like the shadows of night fleeing before the arrows of dawn; and having dispossessed the dark-skinned, the lawless, the godless, the fair-skinned Noble People entered in upon their lands and made them theirs. With them the Noble People brought their Gods of Heaven and Earth, and these they worshipped with sacrifice and ritual and chanting of mantra and offerings of cows and grain and ghi and all the savours dear to hovering divinity. And in peace and plenty their Maharaja ruled them.

Very fair was the city on the banks of bright Rohini. As there were few men of arrogant, dominant riches, so was there no piercing poverty, and, since life was simple, all had enough. The streets were clean-swept and watered, and parks and gardens lay about them where men might shelter in the great heats, and the gay, golden-skinned children played beside the river and grew sleek and round on their food of pure rice and plantains and milk from the deep-dewlapped cattle that wound home in the evenings from high pastures by running water.

Nor was there fare only for the body Wise men, the Wanderers, they whose minds are fixed on things unearthly and whose souls climb toward keen stars as the cragsmen follow the eagle to her eyrie above the clouds, came in from mighty forests where the hermits and their families dwell in peace with God and man pursuing the purities of the householder's life in the wilds ;—bringing with them the dreams, the speculations, the conclusions of the hermits and themselves. And for such the Raja had made a hall of cedarwood in the city, where they might hold disputations with its wise men and the simpler folk sit and listen, bestowing applause or condemnation as they heard. For there was none in the city, gentle or simple, noble or humble, but set the things of the spirit above the chaffer of the market place and lent a ready ear to such talk. Nor did they fear to speak, for the Arya are free peoples, coming from the north, and bold and adventurous.

And of these Wanderers the people learnt much, for if the clansmen were free, these were freer. No love of earthly homes or riches held them. Strip one of them of his worldly all—his tattered robe and bowl for alms—and he would depart content, smiling his strange secret smile, as a man whose treasure is beyond thief or destroyer. But for the *Wasa*, the three months' rainy season, they would stay, willing to speak or to hear, satisfied with a very little, and when the sun shone again, depart like migrating birds on their mysterious way. And sometimes would come one, God-intoxicated, utterly heedless of men, scarce emerging from *samadhi*, the mystic ecstasy ; and him would men surround with mute envy because in that trance he beheld things not lawful nor possible to be uttered. And such would stay but a little while and then, heedless of rain or sun or wind or snow, press on to the cold glories of the mountains, alone and in haste, and reappear no more.

So does the flame of the Divine draw the moth of the spirit of man to hover about it until, dazzled and drunken with radiance, it joins itself to the flame and is consumed into pure light.

Yet was not the talk of the City of Kapila for ever of things divine, for bygone Rajas and this one also (knowing that where there is a North-man he must still be talking and much trouble thereby averted) had made a Folk Mote, a meeting hall, and not one only where in the different quarters of the town men might gather and talk of their affairs, the farmers and handicraftsmen alike,—the sowing and harvesting of rice, the well-doing of cattle, the doings of the Kosalans, of whom they themselves were a clan, the subjugation of the swarthy natives among whom they lay as pearls in a black ocean, the ambitions of the Kings of Maghada, the trading of the merchants, and many things more which concerned them nearly. And each householder had the right to be heard, for each in his own house was king and priest and there none might say him nay, were it not that the Brahmans made or unmade his peace with the Lords of Heaven through gifts and sacrifices and a ritual grown exceedingly heavy and burdensome. But against these even the fair-skinned people, the Arya, as they called themselves, did not as yet dare to murmur.

The women of Kapila also were wives and mothers of free men. Their faces were not veiled save when they themselves for modesty chose to draw the folds between themselves and too bold a gaze. They shared the joys and sorrows of their men, though the great ladics were screened. And if they walked in the ways of ritual piety even more eagerly and laid daily gifts even more precious at the feet of the Brahmans, this is the way of women all the world over.

And these happy people had a good Maharaja, named Suddhodana, or Pure Rice, because not only were his granaries and those of his fathers before him full to overflowing, but his heart was pure as the grains of living pearl; a man grave and kind, rich also in cattle and elephants, yet not arrogant with riches, charitable, alms-giving, reverencing the Brahman and the ascetic, walking in peace in the way of ancient pieties, with thoughts of his own to think as he raised his eyes to the mountains, awful in the heavens as intermediaries between men and Gods. And he had taken to wife two fair sisters, the elder, Maya, the younger, Prajapati; and by the elder, the more dearly loved, had as yet no child and by neither a son to succeed him on his peaceful seat of rulership. And this was a grief to him, for when he was gone who should sacrifice to his soul and the souls of the great dead fathers? Very sweet and grateful is the tenderness of daughters, but this they cannot do.

And one day, as they sat in the pleasure pavilion beside the waters of Rohini, listening to her song of the snows as she danced onward, downward from the heights, the Maharaja Suddhodana opened his heart once more to his wives. And one, Maya the Maharani, sat at his feet on a cushion of silk woven with gold, and her beauty was calm as the evening star shining in a faint moonlight, luminous, remote, veiled with dreams and hopes unknown to others. The second Queen, Prajapati, was fair and gentle, and no more—yet that is much, as shall be shown. And these two were sisters in heart as in blood and wifehood. So, laying his hand on the head of Maya, the Maharaja spoke softly:

"What dreams my Queen?"

And she, pointing to the bamboo grove where stood in green shade a deer with her fawn beside her, said with a slim hand clasping her sister's:

"Of motherhood. Of this I dream night and day, knowing many beautiful things, but most of all this—that the heart of my lord, my beloved, cannot rest until a son of his is laid in his arms. O would, if I am barren, that my heart's sister, my Prajapati, might give to our husband this gift of gifts!"

And he, with heavy brows:

"Dear lady and wife, the Gods give and withhold their great gift of life at pleasure. What have we left undone? We have besought them. We have offered of our best on many an altar. We have fed Brahmans, we have kept the precepts, and yet—they do not give. If in some former life we have sinned—Yet who can tell? It is their will, and must be borne even if it break my heart."

Then Prajapati, raising her sweet eyes timidly to him, her hand clasping her sister's:

"If my lord please to take another wife, then indeed my sister and I will serve her, and if a son is born, what can we but rejoice?"

And he:

"That son would not be the child of my Queens, and most of all of Maya, the Great Lady. Dear he might be, but not so dear; and, moreover, you both, my ladies, have heard the word of the wandering Rishi, the wise ascetic, who prophesied that in this city, in this fortunate palace, should a child be born, a ruler of men, a King among Kings."

"May it be here and now!" said the lady Maya. And again, softly: "May we be found worthy!"

There was a long silence and only Rohini, the river, talked of sweet secret things as she went her way. And presently the Maharaja added:

"I think it will not be!"

And a large tear pearled itself on the long lashes of Prajapati and spilt down the bloom of her cheek as she watched her baby daughter in the arms of a dark-skinned nurse lulling her to sleep with strange and wistful songs of the native people, by the lotuses on the great marble tank in the shade of the pippalas.

And presently the evening came, gliding with silent steps through the woods and along the waters, veiled as a maid who steals to meet her star-eyed lover. And having beheld the pomps of sunset, the mountains withdrew into their mysteries and a star stood on each of their summits for guard, and in a great peace the moon floated upward, resplendent. Then the beauty of heaven and earth became marvellous and remote, and the earth was no longer for men but Gods.

Now that night Maya, the Great Lady, asleep beside her lord in the pleasure pavilion when moonlight blanched the dewy lawns to snow, dreamed a dream. Nor was it the first. This lady was vision-haunted. Her eyes, her ears, were open to all the starry influences, to all the weeping of winds and the tales the reeds whisper to one another in lonely places. But this dream came, not flitting ghostly along the ways of sleep nor with the morning dissolving cloud-like, illusive, scarcely to be grasped or recorded, more a feeling than a thought, but clear, majestic, terrible and beautiful, so that she found herself (and knew not how) sitting up, awake, aware, breathless, as it were a Queen to whom has been made a great annunciation from equal powers. And, with an awakening hand laid upon her husband, she spoke, nor did her voice tremble:

"Beloved, awake! I have dreamed. For it seemed

to me that the four Guardian Divine Kings lifted me from my bed and bore me away to the great mountains and laid me down. And heavenly spirits, shining as stars, came about me and bathed me in the pure waters of a mountain lake, freeing me of all human stain. And when this was done they laid me down again, clothing me in the gold of divine garments and shedding perfumes about me. And I saw a lordly elephant, white as silver, wandering beneath the trees. For, as you know, this is the symbol of royalty. And touching me on the right side with his trunk, he appeared to melt into a cloud and pass like a vapour into my womb. In the darkness I have seen a great light shine, and in the air myriads of radiant spirits sang my joy. And O, beloved, all is well!"

And he stammering, amazed:

"Beloved, when you awaked me, the music of these very spirits rang in my ears, and they cried to me with voices more tunable than all songs of birds or harmony of well-touched lutes, 'The child shall be born when the Flower-Star shines in the east.' And as you touched me, I awoke."

And more they could not say, but clung to each other, trembling for joy and wonder. Nor could any sleep come to them that night, for in their gladness it seemed they stood on the shining shores of heaven, its light about them like an ocean. And when on the morrow these dreams were told to Prajapati, she rejoiced with them, no thought of envy to cloud the crystal of her soul. And when they were laid before the dream-readers, they could presage nothing but good, and being called in before the Maharaja where he sat in state with his Maharanis, they spoke as follows:

"A lord of men shall be born, a great and awful ruler. Let the soul of the Maharaja be exalted, and the heart of the Maharani rejoice and triumph, since to their house is given a son whose kingdom is the earth and the fullness of it."

Then the Maharaja shouted for joy, while Maya the Maharani listened with dreaming eyes.

"For he shall conquer the earth!" he cried, "and the trampling of his elephants be heard like thunder, and Kosala shall be his kingdom and Maghada prostrate before his feet, and riches and glory shall be the slaves of the Conqueror for ever and ever!"

And the Maharani said:

"For ever and ever? Yet there is death."

And Prajapati hid her face.

And the dream-readers, looking up with reverence where they knelt before their diagrams and circles, answered:

"Great Lady, there are riches that Death cannot thieve. There are conquests that Time does not triumph over. There is an Empire that passes not away. What the fate of this child is to be we cannot yet tell. It bewilders us, for great and auspicious as are the signs, they are not plain reading as is the custom. It may be that the child shall be a sage, dominating the souls of men, ruling by pure wisdom, a conqueror——"

But here the Maharaja broke in, in anger:

"Be silent, for this I will not have! The men of my race are Kshatriyas, warriors. The Brahman, the ascetic, the hermit, have their sacred uses, and may the guardian Gods forbid that I should disparage their merit—but my son is my son and a warrior, and if the signs are great, it is a warrior's greatness I claim for him, for in my family is no other known or considered."

But still the dream-readers lingered in doubt.

"Great sir, there is more to be told, strange and very wonderful. Two ways lie before the child to be, and in which he will walk we cannot say. If, when he is of age to judge, he beholds a sick man, an old man, a dead man, and a holy monk, then great and wide is his kingdom but not of this world. And if he see not these signs, he shall be a king of the earth, magnificent in riches, glory and power. Therefore it is in the hand of his father to choose what he shall see or not see. The dream is read."

"Gladly and gloriously is it read!" shouted the Maharaja. "No such sights shall my son see. Leave spiritual things to spiritual men, for he shall reign for ever and ever!"

And bowing, with minds perplexed, the dream-readers gathered up their calculations and departed. And in the city they spread their news, and there was scarcely a man but thought and rejoiced with the Maharaja, commending him in that he chose rather to have a son to fight beside him and ride terribly at his bridle rein than an ascetic in the woods, with matted hair and clawed hands, to pray for his victories—"So would we all choose, like men!" they said. And very joyful was the city.

But Maya the Great Lady, saying little, went her way in peace, strong and calm of purpose as our general mother the earth, pure within and without as the white lotus; and surrounding herself with a great tranquillity, she floated on its surface as a water-lily, rooted in the life-giving bosom of earth, turning an adoring face to the purities of the heavens and absorbing their radiance, until her heart was pure gold and her body white as the ivory of the flower that is a prayer embodied and throne of all the Gods. And if she passed through the city, the women and children strewed flowers before her as before a goddess borne in procession, and when the benediction of her eyes fell on them, they prostrated themselves.

And always her sister, Prajapati, went beside her, guarding her with her own hands, treasuring her as a thing already enskied and sainted, a fear in her heart clasping hands with joy. And the Maharaja Sudd-hodana would stride into the pavilion, saying in his great voice:

"Wife, how goes it? For the time passes onward, and soon the spring shall be here again, and with it our boy. This day have the farmers given me a little plough, made of red cedarwood, banded with ivory, and when he can walk and talk he shall plough his furrow like a man!"

And she, smiling, answered:

"Dear lord, he shall plough his furrow and sow his seed, and very great shall his harvest be. All goes better than well."

And again another day he came with a sword, the haft sparkling like frost with jewels, and he cried, rejoicing:

"This have the goldsmiths and handicraftsmen of the city given me, that with it my son may strike off the head of the goat for his first sacrifice, and after destroy his enemies as when Indra thunders and lightens from the peaks. But is all well?"

And she, smiling:

"Beloved, his enemies shall fall before him like chaff driven on a gale. And all goes better than well."

And she spent her time in deep meditation, free from grief or pain, free also from illusions and desires, in a measureless content and foreseeing. Thus the time went by, not swiftly as a dancer nor slowly as a mourner, but in a great quiet, pacing with majesty from day to day.

Now, on a certain day when Spring with her birds and blossoms was come to earth, the Maharani, following the custom of the ladies of her race, with her sister made ready all her matters and entered the presence of her husband, speaking thus:

"Dear lord, it is a habit of my people that when our children are born it is in the house of our parents. Have I then your permission to journey to them for this auspicious birth, that, returning, I may bring my sheaves with me?"

And he, embracing her with true affection, gave her leave to go, commanding her to the care of Prajapati, and giving strict command that men should go before making all the ways clear for her litter, and men and women be warned that no sight painful or terrifying should meet her eyes. So, tenderly invoking the prayers and ritual of the Brahmans on her and his son's behalf, he sent her forth and returned to his duties full of thought. But she, borne in her litter and embraced in the very arms of peace, went her way, thinking to reach the house of her parents and knowing not that the great hour of her life was even then upon her.

And passing the Lumbini gardens, where trees and flowers, placid waters and green shades, the song of birds and cooing of doves combine to make a heaven on earth, she commanded them to stay her litter that she might set her feet in the sun-warmed grass and stand beside the coolness of the lake. So it was done, and leaning on the arm of Prajapati, she descended and entered the garden and wandered awhile, silent for joy.

And suddenly, as they stood beneath a great palsa tree, sweeping the sward with robes of green and the honeyed snow of blossom, awe and trembling seized her and a measureless marvelling; and the tree swept its boughs earthward until the leaves and flowers lay thick upon the grass, and she knew that the life of all growing things and of the divine earth and the mountains and skies lived within her and that her hour was come. So she laid her hand on a bough of the palsa tree, and as Prajapati knelt beside her, stilled with joy and fear, and her women crowded outside the close blossomed shelter of the palsa tree, her son was born: not like a human birth with agony but painlessly.

Now, it was told afterwards that for wardens the Four Heavenly Kings stood about him, and that the air was thronged with those birds of heaven, the happy Shining Ones, singing and rejoicing. And it is told that throughout the world all polluted streams flowed clear as crystal, and that even as the lady his mother suffered no pang of childbirth, so all sentient creatures knew surcease of pain because of that great Birth and rejoiced with her in jungle and meadow, in deep waters, and in clouds aerial—for what mother or child could sorrow in that hour?

## CHAPTER II

BUT of the child, what shall be said? Borne back to the palace with flute and drum, through streets thronged with eager men and women pressing forward to behold him, he did not sleep, nor shrink, like other children, but gazed about him as though the gem of thought were hidden beneath the blue deeps of his eyes. He shone like pure gold, after the manner of his people, Aryan, noble, a child of high descent. And it is told that the hidden sweetness of precious lilies went with him, and that the garments of shining spirits, sweeping unseen above him, made the air vibrant. So the Maharaja, receiving him in his arms, blessed his son, rejoicing in his happy fate who was the father of such a one as the world could not show the like. And in his ears the voices of prophecy made a changing music of pride and triumph. And the Maharani, overweighted with gladness, like a lily surcharged with dew, was borne to her noble couch of ivory and gold; and Prajapati watched each breath she drew, so great were her love and fear.

Then, to the rejoicing palace, came an ascetic of pure life and understanding, a dweller on the holy heights of Himavat, a great marvel-worker, honoured of all men; and he desired to enter the presence of the Maharaja and make obeisance. And this was granted.

Bowing before the Maharaja, he addressed him thus:

"Great sir, as I came on the sun's way, I heard the

rejoicing of radiant spirits in the air, and when I asked why they were glad, they triumphed in this verse—

"'The Wisdom-Child, that precious Jewel, unmatched, unrivalled,
Is born in Lumbini, in the land of the happy Sakyas,
For good and joy to all the world of men.'

Therefore am I come. Lead me now to the young child that I may see him and be glad also. Rejoice, O Maharaja of happy fortune, for most surely is it owing to your righteous deeds in former lives that this good celestial is fallen to your lot!"

And the Maharaja, dumb with love and pride, led the way to the palace hall where the child slept; and they uncovered his little lovely person that the old man might see and be glad also. So he considered the precious marks and signs of his body, assuring him to be a Buddha, one perfect in enlightenment, reading and comprehending them all with a heart that scarce for joy could believe what lay before him. And, seeing these wonderful birth-portents, the tears rolled down his cheeks; and at his weeping fear seized the father, and he bowed down at the ascetic's feet, crying:

"O, what is my lord's grief: O, what are his tears? Is the child doomed? Do we lose him? Forbid it, all-seeing Divinities! Forbid it that one parched, within reach of the eternal draught, should lose all and perish of thirst! Forbid it that I should lose my treasure! For when a man dies who owns a son, it is as a man with two eyes—one sleeps yet the other watches,—but a man without a son is blind in death's darkness."

And the ascetic, seeing his grief, answered swiftly:

"Sir, have no fear. Good and better than good are the portents. I wept for myself. This child shall rule the world, but I, by reason of my age, shall not live to see it. Deep and full and wide is the river of his Law. Like a great lake is the calm of his Yoga; like the sun at the zenith his wisdom. The earth shall be glad for him, and he shall reign and he SHALL reign, and mighty the glory of his dominion!"

And having said this, the ascetic departed mysteriously after the fashion of the Instructed, leaving joy as his gift.

But still Prajapati watched by the Queen Maya and leaned her ear close to catch a whisper—for as yet the Great Lady had not spoken.

And now the child lay in the hollow of her arm, and it was the seventh day. And without raising her lashes, she whispered:

"Sister, my true sister! On the seventh day I die, for so it is with those mothers whose joy, too great for the lowlands of earth, soars like a bird to the mountains of heaven. My joy is winged. No more can it walk beside my sweet sister nor follow my husband as his shadow nor guard the steps of my child. It is become divine. Already its wings quiver for flight. But all is well. My place is prepared in a heaven where my bliss, rolling outward, may spread into a sea to mirror the Wisdom I have borne. And you, my true sister, will not forget me, but, taking this child for your own, will nourish him with noble milk from your pure bosom. And for our lord you will take heed. And this I know, that the Way of Peace shall be opened to the feet of my son's foster-mother as to mine."

And Prajapati pressed her cheek against the Great Lady's in silence that laid a finger on the lips of grief, and the child slept between them.

Now Night, with the moon in her hair and the stars for ear and breast jewels, came gliding down from the high mountains and wandered in the palace gardens, shedding sleep unutterable and all sweet influences from her outspread hands. And there was not one in the palace, from the Maharaja to the sweeper, but slept dreaming auspicious dreams.

And in the morning all woke refreshed and at peace. But Maya, the Great Lady waked not. And her sister, the Queen Prajapati, seeing the child, lovely as an image of pure gold, blue-eyed and beautiful, loved him, and took him to her fragrant bosom, and became his mother. And he received the name of Siddhartha, meaning, "He who has attained his aim"—for who could doubt that such a child must conquer where he would?

Thus have I heard.

With this child all good came to the City of Kapila and to the country round about, and all the Sakya clansmen prospered very greatly. Their cows were pure-coloured, well-proportioned, giving fragrant and rich milk with even flow; their horses were as though winged, shaped for speed and strength; their elephants royal beasts and understanding. When rain was needed the air distilled it seasonably, and the five cereals swelled with scented grain, wholesome and soft for food. All creatures about to produce their young were content and at ease, their bodies well knit and healthful.

Nor was this grace confined to the lower creation, for in the City of Kapila and its dominions, amongst men and women auspicious things grew like seed flung from the hands of Gods, and even those whom their passions spurred down the broad way of a dangerous karma, considered and took heed, and, laying aside their selfish desires and covetousness, thought no proud, envious thoughts, but lived in quiet with their neighbours; and men were grave and re-collected and women chaste and calm, and by all were Four Rules of Purity honoured. And it is told that the Maharaja, seeing this heavenly guest within his palace, for his sake dwelt purely, practising virtue, putting away from him all evil company, that his heart might not be polluted with lust. And he meditated much by night and day, drinking the moon's brightness with clasped hands and sacrificing in the golden silences of the dawn, when all high influences are unloosed. And this course of conduct must ensue from such a birth, for, as the lotus and champak flowers exhale their perfume and the moon drops camphor in her secret glories, so do the influences of purity and high thought spread outward from the person of a Buddha-to-be. Therefore, as the light of sun or moon increases little by little and none can measure its growth, so was it with the child, orbing into beauty perfect and yet more perfect—if such a thing can be. And with precious things they surrounded him. Noble amulets guarded his person, great gems adorned him, and the scent of sandalwood made sweet the air for his breathing.

Now, when the time for instruction came, the Maharaja considered whom he should employ to teach his son. Should it be a man of the Wanderers, who, having cast the world utterly aside, scans its wisdon with the diamond ray of perfect comprehension—one of the Unfettered? Or should it be one of the men of braided hair—a Brahman hermit, held, as yet, in family ties, but living the life of pure contemplation? Or a bearer of the Triple Staff?

Much he revolved these matters and, gathering opinions, digested them, and summoned to the high task the wise and saintly Viswamitra. And the boy was brought before him and made due obeisance to his teacher (who is, if possible, more to be reverenced than even a father, being the father of the soul and mind, whereas that other may be but the father of the transitory body); but when Viswamitra questioned the noble child, it has been told that there was nothing he did not know already. For it is related that he was familiar with all that has been written in books or told with tongues, even from the number of the spheres and heavenly bodies, as also their triangular, square and sextile aspects, to the powers of the lowliest worm that creeps upon the earth, unable even to raise its head to adore the divine luminaries. There was nothing that teacher could teach him, for already he knew all So Viswamitra heard and trembled, and at last, seeing that this matter touched on things deep, incomprehensible and wonderful, he prostrated himself before the child, and, in all humility, went his way marvelling.

Yet let it not be thought that the Maharaja Suddhodana could behold these portents with a heart of ease, for mingled with all his pride and joy was fear. His son moved before him, beautiful exceedingly, perfect in duty not only to his father and his foster-mother, Prajapati the fair and noble, but also to all with whom he had to do, quick to smile and reply, glad in a boy's sports and games, and yet—apart. As a man, looking down through the clear crystal of a lake, may behold beneath it groves of strange leafage where silver fish dart and disappear in a life unknown to him, so the Maharaja, looking through the translucence of his son's eyes uplifted to his, knew that they revealed yet hid a world in which he had no part. And this aloofness grew to be to him a knife driven into his very heart. And time passed, and the child became a noble youth.

One day the Maharaja sent for his minister, an old man, wise and instructed, and to him he said:

" Is all well in the city and the country about it ? "

And the old minister, saluting, replied:

" O Maharaja, all is well. And since the birth of your auspicious son how could it be otherwise? For it appears that in past times when a child of pure brilliancy was born, there prevailed great prosperity, and wickedness came to an end. And so it is now."

And, sighing as if his heart were like to break, the Maharaja replied:

"This is true. And who should rejoice more than I? Yet it is not so, and my heart is consumed with anxiety."

But the minister remained respectfully silent, and the Maharaja continued:

"For my son is not as the other young nobles, free and gay and enamoured of sports and battle and women, but the opposite—rather enduring than sharing the frolics suited to his age; and when I see him meditating beneath the rose-laurels and mark his calm, abstracted eyes, it recalls to me the saying of the sage Asita, that 'embarking in the boat of wisdom, he shall save the world from peril.' Now, were this to be the wisdom of a great King delivering his people, I might triumph as I did in hearing it, but if it is to be the cold wisdom of the Wanderers and forest-dwellers, then I desire none of it, for to embark in that boat is to be severed from power and from all things dear and desirable to the heart of man. What, then, is your counsel?"

And with grief written in his face, the aged minister replied:

"Great sir, who shall challenge Fate and the unwritten laws of the Divine? I will own that sometimes in the noble youth's presence I have felt as it were a cold air blowing between him and me, as though he stood apart from lesser men. And more than once this thought has occurred: Suppose this noble Siddartha is a Bodhisattva, destined in his next re-birth to be a Buddha, how then shall we fight against a destiny so great and awful? But yet it may not be thus, and so rarely does a Buddha appear upon the earth that there is neither experience nor knowledge to guide us."

And, trembling, the Maharaja replied:

"You voice my very fear. It is certain that many of the predictions which my soul applied to earthly glory, may be read otherwise if considered. But since I dread this unspeakably and we are by no means certain of the end, what is your counsel that we may divert him and so fulfil his mind with beauty and bliss, that these cold visions may blow away like mists at sunrise and leave him glad?"

Then, smiling subtly, the old man answered:

"There is one way, and one only. For it is acknowledged throughout the three worlds that there is no charm of forgetfulness like the beauty of a woman. On her bosom the Gods are forgotten and the wisdom of the wise is vanity."

But the Maharaja, with impatience:

"This is true of others, but as for my son, he has seen the loveliest face to face and has never turned to look again. Think better, old man.'

And he:

"For the noble, a noble bait. And there is a girl, daughter of the great Suprabuddha, young and lovely as the Maiden of the Dawn when she stands, rose-fingered, smiling upon the mountain peaks, and this maiden is pure in health and person, constant and faithful, cheerful evening and morning, one to establish the palace in purity and quiet, full of dignity and grace. Among her companions she moves as the queen swan leading the flotilla, with stately neck, yet bowed in humility. For a King of all the earth this is a fitting consort. I have made diligent inquiry. Her name is Yashodara."

And the Maharaja replied with joy:

"In this Yashodara may be our deliverance! Send in haste, but with dignity, to Suprabuddha her father, and call a gathering at which the bridegroom-to-be shall show his strength with bow and sword and horse gainst all rivals, after the manner of the free choice of our women."

And the old man bowed and went away, smiling, but with a sore doubt at his heart—for he also recalled the words and portents of the Prince's birth and dreaded the anger of awful Gods if any should let their purpose.

Thus on a certain day the lists were set, and the Sakya lords were challenged by the noble Siddhartha to archery, to sword-play and to riding, that the maiden, Yashodara, might know she chose no craven to be her husband. And all the people crowded to see, some wagering on the success of this lord and some on that, but all, on whomsoever they wagered, hoping that the son of the good Maharaja might win honour and the bride. Yet most believed that the victor would be Devadatta, cousin of Siddhartha, a young prince proud and obstinate and amorous and very skilful in feats of arms.

It was in the golden silence of very early morning when the people crowded to the *maidan* where all should be done, for the heat of the later day forbade it then. So still was it that not a frond of the palms stirred nor even a bamboo leaf lifted on the air, and the dew lay bright as silver upon grass and flower. So still that the voice of Rohini, full-throated from the melting snows, would have filled the quiet but for the myriad shufflings of bare feet through the dust and the tinkle of litter bells as the hidden beauty and her companions were borne to the place of meeting. For her face should not be seen until she made her choice.

And all the way was strewn ankle-deep with flowers, as though the Spirits of the Air had rained them with both hands upon the glad earth, and from their bruised beauty was shed such sweetness on the dew that the fragrance rose like incense to greet the lovely ones on their way.

But when the rival lords rode on to the *maidan* in splendour of armour jewelled and inlaid with gold and swords that flashed like lightning from the rifts of cloudy mountains, and horses that seemed to spurn the ground with their hoofs and desire to ride the air like the very coursers of the sun, then the joy of the people so grew that they clapped their hands and shouted lustily, for of all things the noble fair-skinned Northern peoples love a good man and a good horse, and only next to these a beautiful woman. And of the last the most beautiful as yet was hidden. So they shouted until their voices were like the noise of a great wind and the echoes returned them from far-off heights and woods.

And Devadatta rode a horse so black that in the night he seemed a part of it, but Siddhartha's horse was white, proud and great and gentle, and his name shall not be forgotten while the round world holds, for he was Kantaka—and of him more hereafter. And when the maiden, looking between the curtains of her palanquin so that none might know she looked, saw the young Sakya lord, her heart left her bosom and fled into his, settling there like a bird nestling with feet and wings, for there was none like him—none. With calm he sat his horse, awaiting the moment, and young he was and slender and like an image of pure gold, and his eyes were blue and dark after the manner of his people, and his lips and cheek shaped by a great graver. He carried his head as a stag in the spring season, and for all his slenderness was he tense and eager as a bow in the hand of the Brahma King with the arrow laid on the string. And so he waited, and his eyes never sought the palanquin where was hidden the Pearl of Victory. And to her sick heart she said:

"He is not mine! He is above me. What woman can cloud the serenity of those eyes? How can the fiery dart of Madhu, the God of Love, pierce that breast, guarded with the snow of high thoughts? He is a King too high for me—too high."

And it is true that the noble youth thought little of the maiden, but much of the great clash with his rivals, for he knew well that Honour was the prize of the day and that his father's heart must needs break if he failed before all the Kin of the House and the people.

Now it is certain that of this jousting many tales have grown up, of arrows flying miraculously, winged by eager Gods, of sword-strokes such as the world has never seen nor shall see, of horses that the Wind, Vaya himself, might bestride for swiftness and cruel, dangerous pride. And how all this may be I know not, who was not there; but this I know, that Siddhartha was better than the best in all the tests, and that the people stormed and shouted and laughed and wept, knowing not what they did so only they might hail him conqueror, while he stood leaning on his sword, breathing lightly and resting, for the first time smiling, a very splendid young knight.

And the Maharaja, scarcely daring to look in his son's face lest he should too openly show his pride and joy, said only:

"Son, you have done well." And, turning, "Bring forth the bride."

Then all the people were of a sudden silent, that not a word, not a sound of that Beautiful should be lost. And they drew back the pictured curtains of the litter and she stepped forth, most resembling the silver moon floating through clouds to her unveiling and pure radiance and so stood before the people, clad in supple silver that flowed about her like water and jewels that dripped glory braided among the silk-soft hair that fell to her ankles and crowned her brows. (Yet none could look at her splendour, for her face drew the bees of all glances to the honey of its sweetness and there held them, dizzy with ecstasy.) Thus, with a maiden only less fair, on either side, she paced towards Siddhartha where he sat motionless on his white horse as a man of marble, carrying in her hand the Garland of Choosing. And coming before him, she raised her eyes to his and stood silent; but her look pleaded.

Then for the first time he knew in the solitude of his heart the drawing near of another. And soft spring airs came before her, with the singing of mating birds, and pearling of young buds and delicate tremble and thrill of life in green silences and all the good things of this world. And it troubled his calm, because he knew not what it meant, and it was more pain than pleasure. This sweet melody, as it were of flutes and lutes, that came from the tattling of her anklets and the rustle of her garments, overpowered the austere, high voices that had breathed in his ear from birth, and they were silent. Like a man bewildered, he dismounted from white Kantaka, with his arm still laid along the noble neck, and gazed down upon her, and their looks met and were one.

So she stooped and took the dust from his feet, then rising, stately as a young palm-tree, she put the Garland of Choosing about his neck and together they faced the shouting people and the rivals, some sullen as Devadatta the evil-hearted, some glad in the victory as Ananda the Prince, his true cousin.

And of all men who saw that sight be sure that none more beautiful could ever meet their eyes than the silver bride hand in hand with the golden lover, shining as Surya the Sun rejoicing to run his course; for with the touch of her hand, doubt dropped from him like a garment and they were submerged, he and she alike, in the joy of the bridegroom and the bride.

And the Maharaja, laughing aloud for triumph and gladness, said to the old minister:

"We have caught our bird! Thanks be to the God of Love!"

But the old man replied:

"Great sir, it will need the triple cord of love to bind him—your own, the wife's and the child's. Let us wait. Still are we not secure."

## CHAPTER III

THUS have I heard.

Time went by, but since he had snared his bird, the Maharaja Suddhodana resolved that the fetters should be gilded, and calling his minister again, he said to him:

"If a man would cage a bird of heaven (and such, I think, is my son), it is necessary that earth should be made heaven, so that no home-sickness for the blue heights should take him. And because a young man may weary of one woman's beauty, however beautiful, let fresh faces be found to make for him a wreath of such roses of the earth as may intoxicate him with its love and perfume. Send north to Savatthi and south to Benares, and fetch such beauties, such players on the vina and sitar as sing before the high Gods, such dancers as those whose white limbs, melting to music, enchant their eyes. Give orders to build him a house for the winter, when the snow is blue in the hollows of Himalaya and the rivers are locked in his cold heart. See that it be warm and silent and that no wind may creep in, and let white furs of snow-leopards, clouded with black, lie about it, soft and smooth to the touch, and let there be story-tellers to speed the long nights with jest and amorous tale and clash of battle. Shut out the cold and terrible moon with close lattice-work and rich curtains, for she, remote and small in the blue, profound skies, may freeze his soul to the chill calm I fear.

And the minister, saluting, said:

"All shall be done. And yet——"

"And yet there is more before we may sleep in peace. Build for him also a house of spring. Let it be pavilioned and with little stiff, frilled roofs flying outward like the skirts of a dancer when she revolves swiftly. On every point set a wind-bell to resemble her anklets and armlets in their tinkling, so that the soft breezes from the hills shall make an aerial music as they wander about it. Let it appear as if the whole were blown together like a cloud on a wind and might be lifted and dispersed like thistle-down—a dream of spring.

And the old wise man saluted, saying:

"It shall be done. And yet——"

"And yet it is not enough," mused the Maharaja, stroking his great beard. "For we must build also a house for summer—to drowse in, dim and cool and with long echoing colonnades to catch the faintest breath of breeze. Let this house be set in the grass by Rohini, that her liquid voice may sing of the snows when the dog-days are sultry. And let it be paved with shining stone from the mountains, and the walls be of dark cedar carved wonderfully, and all the windows dimmed and latticed that the heats die on the threshold. Choose a place for it where the asoka trees are deep with rich leafage and golden blossom, and the neems spread their shade and the acacias rain white petals and the champak swoons in its heavy sweetness. Let there be a lake, pensive with reeds and green reaches, the haunt of swans and cranes and all beautiful water birds, and silver rills by which my son may sit and muse if he will, until the languor of slowly dropping water shall pass into his veins and be a narcotic binding him for ever to long dreaming days and nights, and he be utterly content.

And the old man saluted, saying,—

"So it shall be done. Is it also your pleasure, Maharaja, that I set a guard at the gate of the park of the three Pleasure Houses?"

And he answered,—

"It is my pleasure. And now I will visit my son's wife and hear her mind."

So he went to the place of the women in the great house. And his presence being told to Yashodara, she came before him, sweet as the star of evening bathed in rosy vapours, for a dress fell about her coloured as though dipped in the blood of red roses and bound with gold that, winding spirally upward round her lovely limbs and bosom, embraced them, drawing the eye to the slender curves, and she wore no jewels but only the great rings in her ears sparkling with fiery gems. And he drew her to his feet and she sat on a cushion beside him, looking upward with duty and affection, waiting for the favour of his speech. And at last, having observed the delicate sweetness of her face and her grace and majesty, he said, sighing:

"Noble daughter, you have now been wedded to my son, Siddhartha, for six months. Is all well with you?"

And, stooping to touch his feet, she replied:

"Great father, all is well. And I did not know that in all the world there was such joy as I share night and day with my dear lord. For beyond all beauty he is beautiful and beyond all goodness, good, and his gentleness of speech is not like that of a woman, but with strength behind it like Himalaya when he smiled in sunshine. And yet——"

The words stopped like hovering birds on her sweet lips and her fine brows drew together as she meditated. And the Maharaja, drawing his hand from her head, leaned forward to look into her eyes.

"Daughter, have you a doubt—and what is it?"

She, lovely and submissive, made haste to answer,—

"Great lord, all is pure joy, and yet——"

And he, in great anger, so that she shrank down, veiling her face with her hands:

"And yet! When I command my minister to surround my son with all joy wherewith to bind and hold him, he obeys, but ends always with 'And yet—' as though some mystery surrounded him! And you, that should triumph in pride and joy, say the like. My son is fair and free and noble and sharer in my riches and pride. What is this miserable 'And yet—' that mocks my hope? Speak out, woman, and tell me what is in your heart."

And, kindling her courage at his sternness, the wife of Siddhartha looked at him with clear, unsullied eyes.

"Father, all I have said is truth, but there is also this. In the midst of rejoicings of song and when the women dance before him and the feast is spread and the great fruits, cooled with snow, and purple wine in cut crystal cups are set to his hand, then often I know that though his fair body is among us, his soul is escaped and fled away."

And in her eyes two tears gathered and stood but did not fall.

And he, with anger:

"Would it not be thought a woman should know her business! For what is beauty but to hold a man prisoner to the senses? And you are beautiful as the woman the high Gods made with flowers—how then do you fail? Does he not love you?"

"Sir, he loves me. But not me only. He loves something that I know not, and his thought flies away to it as a dove flies home."

And he said,—

"True, true! It is true. What is this thing? For I, too, have felt it. When I have spoken of wealth and power and pride, I have known that as you, daughter, say, his soul is escaped and gone, I cannot tell where. But have no fear. Tell me only this—has never a word, never a sight of sorrow crept into the paradises I have made for him ?"

And she answered,—

"Not one. All is joy unceasing."

"And no sign of age, of sickness, of death? For, as I have told you, he must not know that these things are, and until he passed into your keeping, the secret was well guarded."

And she replied gravely:

"The secret is well guarded. He does not know. When he speaks, it is of an eternity of delight and of nothing else. And yet—if I may speak and live——"

And he said,—

"Speak. Even in the words of women there is sometimes wisdom and you are a pearl among women."

"Great lord, is it possible to strive against the high Gods? For they have appointed death and sickness and grief to be our lot, and it may be that the very joy of life is the greater because we know it is brief. Children suck sugar-cane until they sicken, and may not grown man and woman weary of sweet things, desiring to match their fortitude against grief? And he is great of soul."

Then he would not look at her for anger, saying,—

"Folly and double folly—woman's madness! Have you not heard the saying of the wise, that if ever he hears tell of age and sickness and death, his doom is sealed? And mine with it—and mine with it! For I love my son."

Then the great tears overflowed her eyes and ran down like a stream at the thaw.

"Forgiveness!" she cried. "Forgiveness! for I love my husband, and if this unknown sweetness capture and carry him from me, what good should my life do me? But now, most honoured father of my lord, I have a hope—a hope! Will a child's hand hold him?"

And even as the words left her lips, he caught her

two hands and gazed deep into her eyes and triumphed. And he said,—

"Daughter, you are hope, and your words a cup in the desert! For, knowing what my son is to me, I know that those hands will hold him when yours and mine drop helpless. Go back to him and tell him, and to the great Gods do I give thanks because my prayers and sacrifices have not run to waste but are rewarded!"

And as she knelt before him, the tears rolled down his cheeks for gladness, nor could he hide them, as a warrior should.

And, beautiful as a rainbow flowering against a black cloud, the Princess returned to the carved chamber of cedar with its lattices set wide to the perfumed air of summer. Beneath and around them the ivory chalices of the frangipani blossoms and starred clouds of jasmine offered warm incense to the sun and all was calm as heaven, as though the world, captured by the power of Yoga, were in ecstasy, dreaming with open eyes upon Perfection. The leaves of deep-foliaged trees floated on air in absolute stillness, swimming silent, in liquid gold, and below the shades of the gardens gleamed Rohini, she also dancing no longer as in spring, but calm and silent as the meditation of a saint, pursuing her shining way in a deep quiet.

There, seated beneath a neem tree, in the green bower of its heart, the Princess beheld Siddhartha as he sat with his feet folded and his hands lying upon his knees. And as she watched, kneeling by the lattice, he stirred no more than a noble image of himself made in gold and there was that in his calm that struck her soul with fear. Then presently, gathering courage from knowledge of the gladness she bore within her, she rose, and folding the gold sari about her brows, she went with rose-leaf footsteps through the House of Joy, passing those palace rooms where the fair women talked and sang and made low music with their vinas and sitars, eating fruits cooled in blocks of ice from the mountains and laughing with each other as though joy could never cease nor death wreck youth and life, for it seemed that the secret of the house held them also and that they, like the Prince, believed these things were immortal.

But Yashodara, going through the garden ways, past groups of tall flowers bee-haunted, flickered about by rose-coloured and black butterflies, caught wafts of varying perfumes, like strains of music through the opening and closing of celestial doors, so sweet was the world that day. The jewelled peacock and his wife led forth their train of little ones to pace in deep grass and silver pheasants went daintily in the plumed shades of the bamboo and their young followed rejoicing in life and warmth and plenty, and birds hidden in high branches sang as if never they would cease, and above all floated the blue sky—a blue pure and strong as that of the infinite ocean, and life and love wandered hand in hand along the blossomed earth in sunlight like clear water. So though her secret winged her feet the Princess must needs pause here and there to share with all these living creatures the wine of joy poured from the sun's brimming cup, and her soul gladdened within her in the youth of the world. And at last with steps light as the fall of a petal she approached the great neem tree and stood and looked into its shade.

Now here was an extraordinary stillness as though an arresting finger were laid upon the pulse of life, but not wholly silencing it, for from a fern-fringed spring there fell at regular intervals a bright drop of water marking time into divisions lest it should wholly slip into Eternity and be lost. And the shade within was deep and green making a soft dusk at noon, and through the shade could be seen the great spires of silver mountains ecstatic in blue air and resembling the highest reach of the aspiration of man arrested on the verge of comprehension.

Very still in green shade sat the son of the Maharaja, his hands, palm upward, laid empty upon his knees, his eyes fixed on the everlasting hills, neither joy nor trouble upon calm brows, lost in meditation so deep that it walled him as in crystal from the fair shows around, and her coming was nothing to him for he neither saw nor heard it.

Then a wave of anguish rose in her bosom and swelled until it spilt in salt and bitter water from her eyes, and she could not restrain herself from that forbidden show of sorrow, and putting aside the boughs she ran to him and fell at his knees and laid her head upon them, sobbing. And with a long sigh he awoke and looked down upon her, smiling.

"What is it, wife, and why do your eyes run like Rohini. Is it a new gladness beyond gladness? And why are you so glad?"

Weeping and sobbing she hid her fair face upon his knees, clasping them passionately, her words stumbling from her lips in agony.

"It is not gladness, O heart of my heart. It is grief."

And he, from the inward Kingdom of Calm.

"And what is grief, my lotus flower?"

For in all his life he had neither heard the word nor seen the thing and she spoke an unknown language. And as she sobbed on, he lifted her face gently in his two hands and looked at her closed eyelids, the lashes wet and matted on her cheek with running tears, she pale as death, the rich colour dead in her lips, and on his beautiful face was amazement and no more, for how could he pity who had lived only in the presence of joy? And at last he said very slowly as if bewildered:

"My rose, my delight, what is this new thing, and

what have you to tell me? Speak that I may rejoice also."

And his words stung some terror in her because he could not understand and it seemed that she must bear the burden of grief and the hidden secret of the world's woe not only for him and herself, but for all the earth. For from any creature born human, though young and beautiful and a Prince, it may well seem a daring too great for mortals to deny grief and affront sorrow and to shut the door in their gray faces—knowing them waiting and watching outside. So the words broke from her sobbing lips :

"This morning I woke, and in the august quiet of the dawn I knew that my hope of hopes was given to me and my joy brimmed and sparkled in the cup of jewelled gold from the Gods, and I would have turned then into my lord's breast to tell of it, but that night you had not passed with me but in the chamber of deodar, so I lay and dreamed awake, lost in bliss until they brought me word that our father would speak with me, and I went."

"But all this was good, my lily swaying on blue waters. And what was your hope?" he said with a hand coming and going softly in her hair, and the monotony and gentleness of his touch soothed her like the immeasurable falling of far-distant water no louder than the humming of a bee. And drawing more quiet breath, she continued :

"Our father asked me, lord of my soul, whether still you escaped away in soul from all the love and laughter about you. For when this is so, is it not that we fail to make you glad, and am not I, your wife, the worst sinner? O heart of my heart, what more is there that we have not done? Tell me, I beseech you."

And he answered, "Nothing," looking above her head to the heights.

Passionately she caught his hands in hers.

"Then, O beloved, if we have done all and fail, *what* is it that draws you from me? What is your soul's desire? When our father, believing a man might weary of my poor beauty, sought out new faces for the Painted Chambers, did I weep? I smiled, though— But no, I will not say it. If it was your pleasure, what should I be but glad? But still you were drawn from us, and it has been a terror that bit into my soul, when waking in a white moonlight, I have seen you sitting with alien eyes fixed upon the great march of the stars. And yet I have kept silence. But now, lord of my life, I ask this —where is it your soul goes, and to whom?"

Her hands, hot with the fever of the soul, pleaded for her, clasping his. Her dark eyes heavy with tears entreated mercy. He answered gravely:

"I go to my own people."

"And we are not your own people? Beloved, beloved— Your words are swords, who then are your own?"

"I cannot tell."

Her hope forgotten, the Princess knelt beside him.

"O noble one, is it life or death that draws you?"

"I cannot tell. What is death? But life such as this is weariness inexpressible, and how men endure it I cannot know. Without change, break, or ripple the sunshiny days glide past, each bringing in its hands the same offering of love and peace monotonous as a dove's cooing. My life is without hope, for, having all, what is there to hope for? And what I have is oversweet. It cloys in the tasting like honey. And the Brahmans make their sacrifices and mutter their mantras of invocation and propitiation, and for what? For if we have all, what more is there to have, and why pray for what is unneeded? If this Paradise over-sweet can never crack asunder; if ages and ages hence we still shall sit here young and beautiful as to-day,—the Gods have emptied their hands and what have they left to give? And if we do amiss, how shall they punish us? And will not the day come when I may lift up my hand to the mountains and curse them, saying—' Be at ease in your careless heavens, O unapproachable Gods,—but I am a man with a soul not to be captured and tamed in earth's paddock. I demand my rights, though what they are I know not, for I move in a perfumed cloud that blinds me. But I shall know one day.' "

She looked up at him in fear that forbade speech.

" I hear the noise of hammers outside the gardens, the cry of the plougher, the song of the maids who come home with cattle from the outer meadows. And I say that these people have lives better than mine, and if I could change I would, for sweet must be their sleep and glad their leisure, but for me life is all idleness and sleep, and their eternity is better than my own. I will ask my father to let me go out and labour in the glad world outside this prison, that buys its food with happy toil, that I too may know what it is to eat the bread I have earned in contentment."

Pale with fear Yashodara answered.

" But, lord of my life, how is it known to you that their life is all good? Is it possible to envy what you know not? "

" I know that with them life is eternal as with me and doubtless joy perpetual. But to this they add useful toil that gives us our luxuries. All these fair things about us are made by the hands of free men rejoicing in beauty. And I make nothing. I pass from one enjoyment to another, fettered—a winged bird in a jewelled cage. Are they not happier than I? And you, sweet wife,—what joy have you in comforting the long hours of a slave? "

She kissed his hands with passion, her black hair falling silken about his feet.

"It is I that am the slave, my King—the happy slave of your beauty and nobleness, and what could I ask but to wait eternally upon your pleasure and that of your son."

He turned his eyes gravely upon her.

"My son?" he said. And she:

"It is true—it is true. And it is because I bear this hope in my bosom that it pierces me like a sword to see your calm averted eyes and know you far away in that strange heaven where I cannot follow. O, my lord, if it be true that you have alien kindred I cannot reach, let your son be of them. Give him all good!"

Then stooping, he drew her head to his breast and put his arm about her and drew her gently until she sat upon his left knee—that throne of the Indian wife, and thus they remained awhile in silence, and his touch was better than speech and his quiet healing as moonlight. Nor did she miss words of love or rejoicing for his calm folded her in the very wings of peace. At long last he spoke:

"My Pearl of Perfectness, we two are one, and of our true oneness springs this new delight. To me the hope is sweeter than all harps touched in the hollow of Heaven. and if you were dear to me before, judge how dear now. But since we are so one, come nearer, share my thought as well as my heart. Does it content you that we should bring into our prison another prisoner and one so dear? Here the days slip by uncounted—a chain of fadeless flowers. Here the river links its long silver thought for ever and ever down the channel from the peaks. Here the bright birds flash by eternally. Will they people the garden to overflowing with their beauty or do they fly away to freer lands as I would if I could? When this garden is full of our children and theirs, what then? Am I the only prisoner or they also? *What* is the secret my father holds from me?"

But she, trembling, could answer nothing. And again there was silence and only the bright slow dropping of the little spring, and her heart forboded sorrow.

" O day of joy made bitter with fear ! " it said within her.

And again he fell into deep cold meditation, and forgot her utterly, and his arm relaxed and slipping fell beside him, and she crept from his knee, and he did not know, staring with lost eyes toward the stainless heavens. And for awhile she stood and watched unnoticed, and then crept shuddering away.

And beneath the shade of the neem Siddhartha sat motionless until the rays from the low sun struck high up the tree trunks, and sunset followed, a breath of rose on a rainbow sky, and presently the moon rose unclouded in luminous loveliness and floated to the zenith, and all boughs dropped dew, and the mountains were lost in stars.

Nor did any dare to break his dream.

## CHAPTER IV

THUS have I heard:

Time went by, each day sweet as new honey dripping golden from a golden comb, sweet, inexpressibly sweet, and the Princess, moving languidly, trembling with hope mingled with doubt and fear, would tell only her joys to the Maharaja Suddhodana and not her fears. For what help was there in him? He could not strengthen the guarding gates, for they were strong and armed men watched by them: nor the walls, for they were high, and observed from watch-towers. And yet, day by day and night by night the spirit of Siddhartha had passed invisible between the swords and unsleeping eyes.

But since the hope of the Princess was made known to him, he shut himself within the great gardens in spirit also. There should no cloud dim the eyes of the mother of his son—flowers must bud and blossom in her heart as about her slender feet, and no thought but peace and security creep into her Paradise. And little by little, as a wild deer glimpsing through the green flies in terror yet may be slowly won with patience and tenderness till it will browse the rose-leaves in a girl's hand, so was the fear of the Princess put to sleep, and a low song of joy and immeasurable thankfulness made music in her heart like the summer voice of Rohini after the melting of the snows—when the river is deep and peaceful.

And one day the Maharaja came to visit her in the cool chamber of roses looking toward the north and the eternal mountains and found her stringing jade and crystal and amber on a fine golden cord, while ladies sat about her plucking rose petals for paste of roses, and there was a sound of far music in the gardens, and looking through the lattice he saw Siddhartha with his best and dearest cousin, the Prince Ananda, shooting with bow and arrow in a wide meadow by the river, and Devadatta and another of the Sakya lords stood by, and the young men laughed and shouted, and their voices came small and clear with distance, so that the heart of the King exulted and he triumphed as he seated himself on the golden and peacock cushions, dismissing the women.

" We have conquered, lovely one ! " he said, laughing kindly in his black beard. " What neither I nor all my sages could do your small wise hands have done, for in them the mother of his child holds my son's heart. I knew—I foretold, it must be so, for he is loving and good and all the pieties of life hold him like bands of iron. You are content ? "

And she, smiling.

" Noble father, I am content. I have no more ' And yets ' with which to wound your ear. My lord leaves me neither by night or day, except when I entreat him to try his strength with Ananda and Devadatta and the Sakya lords. And this is wisdom. We strained too tight upon the fetters and they ate into his soul. This freedom among the young lords is well. My noble father, I entreat you to give him what liberty you can, for it is good. Never now do I see him submerged in the cold dreams that stole him from us. Those strange voices call him no more, the hands have ceased to beckon. He is ours—yours and mine and the child's, and of the child is all his talk and thought. He shall ride with sword and lance and be a King of Kings. So we say—one to the ›ther."

She looked up with tears of pure joy trembling like

shed diamonds on her long black lashes, and the Maharaja, grave with delight, replied:

"So it shall be! What!—the kingdom of Maghada is ruled by a foolish man—the King Bimbisara,—why shall not my son oust him as we gather strength? Ha! are not we too of the Arya—the great fighting people, and may not one elephant subdue another! Daughter, I would have you breathe these things in my son's ear, and thrill him with hope of great splendours for the child"

She answered eagerly:

"Father, I have done—I do it. I say each day—'Give him his inheritance, my lord. Let all good that you gain be his, for he is yours and ours,' and always he replies: 'Could I find the whole world's Pearl it would be for my great father, for you and for the child. Be content, wife, for my heart is with my own people.'"

And as she spoke his words the tears of gladness brimmed and fell on the crystals and jade and amber in her golden lap and the Rajah clapped his hands together and shouted for joy.

"Ha, ha! we have won him! O auspicious daughter, dip your hands in my treasury and take at your will. What reward is enough for your beauty and wisdom? But now be cautious"—[There he became grave and weighty]—"guard your health and your person as the deposit of a King, and all shall be well. And the day is not far distant when we shall laugh at the sickly foretelling that said if he saw death, pain or old age he would flee into the jungle. What! Shall not my son have strength to face the common lot of man like a great King! But not yet—not yet! We will go warily."

And the wise Princess saw that beneath his triumph he was not even yet wholly reassured. But she herself was content.

So when Siddhartha returned flushed and gay from

riding and shooting by the parks of Rohini with the great bow in his hand and quiver at his shoulder, a glittering glorious young warrior, she clung about him shining with bliss so that it appeared that visible rays surrounded her as they do the Dawn Maiden when she, standing, flings her golden arrows about the world from the peaks of Himalaya. And with his arms about her in their chamber of marble he said:

"And is my dove content? And is life good?" and she replied:

"Most utterly content. If life is good to my lord it is delight to me. But you, O, heart's dearest—and are you not content? See how the world is white with blossom dropping perfumed dew, and the blue birds flash through them, and there is piping and singing and the flutter of wings through all the happy gardens and the humming of black-bees mad for honey. And this morning as I walked with Gautami the slender-waisted, close, close hidden in the jasmine flowers I found a small nest—small and heart-holding and in it four blue jewels of eggs warm from the mother's breast—warm as love and home, and blue as the skies, and I looked and said—'One, two, three, four. This is a prophecy. These are the three sons and the one daughter I shall bear to my lord. First—three sons, one by one, and then a daughter so lovely that all Kings of the earth shall desire her, and the three strong brothers shall guard her beauty—that is fit only for the enjoyment of the King of the Three Worlds! And we will hide this lovely one in the heart of the gardens until he comes. Now, since I have seen this portent, four there must be. Less there cannot. But possibly more!"

And she leaned back, flashing the sunshine of her eyes in his, and he laughed back holding her by the two hands, half dazzled with her beauty and gladness.

"This is life," he said—"and the cold dreams are

gone. They rose like mists from Rohini in autumn mornings—and in the rising of the sun they disperse. And the coming of my son has driven them into the night where they belong."

Therefore great gladness reigned in the House of Gardens and doubt was forgotten, and in his pride, willing to make his son more free and yet security more secure, the Maharaja made another and most beautiful garden across the city where Siddhartha might take his pleasure if he wearied of the Gardens of Rohini, and the Princess approved this with her wisdom, saying: " We must stretch the tether, lest the bird guess he is not free to fly into the distances."

And this was a most exquisite garden, with great pools and lakes where white cranes stood meditating all day among blue lotus blossoms—the very essence of the blue of the waters, and it was made a Paradise where none might take life or harm the creatures of earth or air or water, and the wild swans floated as pure and fearless upon those lakes as upon the bosom of holy Manasa in the sky-uplifted bosom of the mountains, and the deer were not shy but walked beside men, and with great eyes, silent though full of speech, told them the hidden histories of their wild hearts.

And on a certain day Siddhartha sent a message to his father.

" Great father, if my Paradise is ready, give me permission to drive through the city to-morrow that I may enjoy it with my cousins Ananda and Devadatta and the Sakya lords."

And the answer returned was " To-morrow," and that night Siddhartha passed with his wife Yashodara in a pavilion of Chinese silks with blue and gold dragons by the banks where Rohini wandered among her reeds singing a little song of sleep, and as the orange sunset faded into gray a few large stars came out, and swam in immeasurable deeps above them. And she said, holding his hand :

" How beautiful—how beautiful is the coming of the night with all the stars caught like bees in her net of blue,—and is it not strange, O lord of my life, to think that long ages after we and our love are forgotten other lovers shall sit by this little river and see the night glide down the mountains scattering stars about the world like seeds of light. Shall we see, shall we know, in those cold other lives they promise '

And he in great astonishment:

" Forgotten ? In what age to come shall you not still be loveliest and gentlest, Queen of the whole earth for beauty ? Then, as now, shall men come to happy Kapila because the city holds the most beautiful as the shell its pearl. How should we be forgotten ? "

And for a moment cold fear crept by her like the silent passing of a snake, compelling her to remember that the truth was shut from those dear eyes, light of her life,—and she brushed it from her and said, laughing,—

" True—who should forget us ? I dream sometimes that of all names in the world my lord's shall be greatest, uplifted, splendid, like that great star throbbing upon the topmost peak of all, and men shall bow down and do homage to it not only in the land of the Sakyas and in Maghada and Kosala, but in the wide great world among strange people who send us their treasures but whose very names we cannot utter."

" And you have dreamed this, beloved ? And how ? "

" I have dreams that beat in my ears and their sound goes over the mountains, north and south and east and west. And the sun is dimmed with fumes of incense offered to a great King. And I see golden palaces like the sands of all the rivers for number, with my lord sitting throned beneath them in gold—palaces innumerable, and flowers cast in heaps to exhale their perfume. And all this in my lord's honour. This have I dreamed four times."

And he said, slowly,—

"It is my dream also. Certainly the Gods come in dream. But who can say? See, beloved, how the night, mother of men, brings us her dark reposes lulling all things to sleep. There is no moon, but strange spirits as white as moonbeams moving among the trees. Sing low to me, beloved, sing low. I would not see their eyes —they look upon me with thoughts I cannot read. Sing to me—fill my eyes with the love in yours. Sing!"

And she took her sitar of ebony and ivory and sang softly as Rohini that made a silver music at their feet.

But there was a seal upon her lips that she might not sing of love though love was beside her, for the awe of the mountains was heavy on them and the listening of night. Therefore she sang these words, but no louder than a bee hovering about a flower:

"The wild swans rise from earth,
Strong in the path of the sun.
How should it give them mirth
With his great day begun?
Upward the white wings fly,
Clouds in the bluest blue,
Far they soar—and high!—
Would I might follow too."

And again after awhile she sang a great hymn of the ancient Scripture but lower still:

"Though difference be none, I am of Thee,
Not Thou, O Lord, of me.
For of the sea is verily the wave,
Not of the wave the sea."

And there was silence, and he turned and laid his cheek to hers and they sat together long, gazing speechless at the marvel of the starry deeps. Nor did they know that their last night of peace was with them.

Meanwhile the commands of the Maharaja went out into every street and house of Kapila.

"To-morrow the chariot of my son goes through the streets to the Paradise of Pleasure. See and beware that no aged man or woman be abroad in the city, for my son's eyes must behold no aged, sick or dead person. It is forbidden by the Powers that rule his destiny. Therefore let none but healthy, glad and beautiful persons fall in his way, for if otherwise the transgressor must die."

And there was not a soul in the place but heard this command, and touching their foreheads murmured. "It is an order." And men, women and children ran busily here and there garlanding the happy streets, and they set up poles gilded and painted and with gay fluttering banners. And dwarfed trees after the Chinese manner were placed along the roads, and there were hanging canopies of blue and rose silk, and magnificent tapestries were hung from the windows, until the city shone beautiful as the Paradise of the Gods on the holy mountain Sumeru, and bands of children running like the lesser angels strewed flowers through all the ways where Siddhartha should pass.

Then steadily as the running of a river the people poured in from the country-side to see their young Prince, and the ways were gay with happy folk dressed in their best and garlanded with garlands of marigolds and little rosebuds scented with fragrant oils to increase their own fragrance. The towers were filled with men and women clustering like bees. The mounds by the trees, the windows and terraces—were thronged with eager persons,—the men looking sharply about them to see that nothing was left which might offend the eyes of the heir. And there was nothing, for in bright sunshine, tempered by a cool breath from the mountains, none but happy and beautiful people with their children rejoiced and were glad.

Now see the glorious chariot of ivory inlaid with gold made ready by the gate of the Garden House, fronted with jewels glittering in the bright challenging sunbeams, spread with noble silks flowered with gold, and drawn by four equal-pacing stately horses, white as the ivory they drew, and harnessed with splendour,—their pride subdued to the pride of their master. And beside them stood Channa, the charioteer, a young man well born and noble in mind and person.

So, having saluted his wife, the Princess Yashodara, the Prince Siddhartha, advancing, ascended the chariot, robed in gold and jewels and appearing like Surya the sun when he blazes at his zenith, and all veiled their eyes from his brilliance.

And as he came through the streets, his horses pacing gently, the people swayed toward him and a whisper of awe and delight ran through them like the breathing of a breeze that blows the blossoms in passing.

Looking upon them his heart exulted with joy and kindness, for he thought—" This is my city of delight. These are my people, and it shall eternally be my bliss to do them good. Look at the strong fathers holding up their little sweet children to see their Prince. Their hearts are full of love even as my own. Look at the lovely mothers with their babes in warm bosoms—only less fair than Yashodara, and full of love and gentleness. And the glorious young men straight and tall, and the antelope-eyed girls with silken hair braided with blossoms. The Gods know it is a happy world with all these noble creatures in it, and my sick dreams of I know not what are dispersed in this bliss and the great joy of my people."

And he saluted with his hands, smiling right and left that none might be forgotten, and sometimes from the chariot he took an armful of flowers and tossed them lightly among the crowd, and they were gathered up with delight and pressed to eager lips and brows because they had touched the Prince's hand. So he went through the city, marvelling why his father had forbidden it hitherto. And as he flung his last handful of flowers the appointed moment struck—predestined by the Rulers,—and across the way of the chariot staggered an old, old man, and the stately stallions arched white necks and tossed their heads in disdain at this revolting sight, for they, too, had beheld nothing but loveliness until that moment.

And because the commands of the Maharaja were stern it is said that this figure was no mortal man but a divinity hidden in flesh whom none could let or hinder and that the myriad people of Kapila saw nothing of this—but two saw clearly—the Prince and the charioteer, Channa. And how this may be I cannot tell. Thus have I heard.

And the aged man with tattered white hair depending from his bleached and bony head like lichen from a stricken tree, supporting his painful steps on a stick, weak, imbecile, skinny jaw fallen disclosing toothless gums, eyes red and bleared, without lashes, and moisture oozing from them, drawing oppressed and painful breath, and terror-stricken amidst the crowds, tottered across the flowery way and sank, heaped and huddled beside the chariot, casting a look of terror upon the radiant Prince, and mumbling and muttering what none could hear, his head shaking like a leaf in wind. And it was as if darkness and terror obliterated the sun and all the crowded people bowed forward to see the stopping of the chariot, breathlessly remembering the Maharaja's commands, but none stirred in his place and even the children were dumb. And yet they had seen nothing but the face of the Prince with a shadow fallen upon it. And the Prince laid his hand on the reins and the horses stopped with drooped crests, and shaken with horror he cried aloud to the charioteer :

" Channa, what is it ? What is this man ? If indeed man it be."

And the old man crouched there, muttering, and great fear held Channa silent, and again the Prince cried aloud :

" What is it ? What is it ? "

And again the crowd sighed like the first stirring of winter winds, and there came answer from Channa's lips where he stood, bowed over the golden reins grasped in his hand.

" Prince, this is an old man. This is old age." And a long sighing sob commoved the crowded people as though their doom were pronounced, when they heard.

But the Prince, the words almost dying on his lips, said, trembling :

" What is old age ? Was this unhappy one born so, or has it fallen as a judgment from Heaven ? "

And again the crowd sighed like the first stirring of winter winds, and Channa, face hidden, replied :

" Prince, he was not so born, nor is it the Gods' anger, but this is the common lot and to every man born on earth it comes nor can it be escaped. This ruin of a man was once a child at his mother's breast, and then a boy filled with laughter and sportive gaiety, a joy to see and hear. Later, a youth, beautiful, amorous and brave, such as attended on bliss, and in enjoyment of the Five Pleasures. But old age, dogging the steps of men as a hound with fell teeth, has dragged him down at last and had its will of him, and he lives a life of pain and men avoid him and women pass him by."

And some women in the crowd wept aloud, and the air was heavy with sighing and the old man moaned and muttered with toothless jaws.

But the Prince, still unbelieving and trembling, said:

" And will this doom come upon my great father ? "

" Noble sir, yes."

" And upon the beauty of—my ladies ? "

" Even so."

" And upon me ? "

And there was a fearful silence like death among the crowd and no word from Channa, so that had a breath stirred in the palms it would have affrighted the soul.

Then suddenly the Prince cried aloud:

" Turn back the chariot. What heart have I for pleasures ! Tear down the garlands. Where is there room for joy ! I have seen what I have seen."

And, wordless, Channa turned the white horses, and guided the chariot along the way it came and the people fell back to make way, and men and women hid their faces like mourners for it seemed as though in the knowledge of the Prince knowledge had come to them also of the terror of life and the doom inevitable.

## CHAPTER V

Now when Siddhartha returned to the Garden House, one ran before him and told the women what had occurred, and the ladies bore the news to the Princess where she waited, and when she heard it, she said:

"O ill-foreboding heart of mine! Did I not know that the anger of the Gods must burn against those who would conceal their righteous doom from any man born upon this cruel earth? For who can fight with fate? If this drives my lord to despair, what shall be done?"

So she sent messages to the Maharaja telling him the danger and went forth into the Painted Hall to seek the Prince, and he sat there alone, surrounded by lovely images painted upon the walls, where joy and triumph and love clasped hands, and dancing limbs shone amongst flowers and all the world was white with spring.

Now something in his eyes held his wife from him and she had no courage to draw near, and went and sat herself humbly on the ground before him but at a distance, and at last he said:

"This was the secret. You knew it and did not tell me."

And in the hall was no sound.

"You saw me fed with lies such as these—" (and he flung out his arm against the pictures) "and you did not tell me they were the mask of horror." She bowed her head upon her hands speechless.

"And I, most pitiable, most ignorant, rejoiced that a son should be given to me, not knowing that such a one is born to a heritage of wretchedness and the inevitable approach of shame and ruin. And from this is no escape, for the Gods have appointed no end to our misery, no door from the prison, but we must live eternally and horribly, old and disgraced in body and mind. Could a man but end it and fall into the dark and be forgotten! O had I known, no child of mine should ever have felt the whip and dragged the chain. I will not blame you who are but a woman,—but my father—my father."

And in the hall was no sound at all. And the Princess, hiding her face, thought, "Shall I tell him of the end—of Death?" But she dared not.

And he called aloud for the women and said:

"Deface these pictures for they are lies, and the sight of them turns the knife in the wound. Blot them out with blackness."

So it was done, but the Maharaja in terror bade them redouble the pleasures of the Paradise and of the Garden House. And at great cost he bought a fair slave from the outlands, golden-haired as dawn, sapphire-eyed as blue ice of the Himalaya, white as the elephant's tusk, skilled in all arts of love, and among the darker beauties of the pleasure chambers she moved radiant as though day had broken forth in starry midnight, and all the neighbouring Kings hearing were envious. And in this beauty all hoped, even the sad Yashodara, and her heart failed her when she saw the Prince's eyes coldly averted from loveliness that might have stirred the eternal Gods. And again she sent a message to the Maharaja.

"Your son, my lord, will not look upon the beautiful white stranger nor on any. O send him forth in freedom, for penned in these sweet gardens he muses and meditates, and what is in his heart I cannot know, but fear very terribly. Yet guard the way that no sad sight approach him, for if he sees more all is lost."

And again orders were given, and as before the Prince

set forth, but this time grave and sad, and the crowds shared his mood and the city could not rejoice.

And as they neared the street all a-flutter with banners and flowers and perfumes and thronged with silent gazing thousands again a divinity masked his divinity in tortured flesh (thus it is told), and by the way was seen a sick man struggling for life in a losing battle.

His body was swollen and disfigured, his hollow cheeks blazed with fever and in his dying eyes fear and agony contended. Scarce could he drag himself along, moaning and crying for pity, the hot tears pouring and searing his cheeks as they ran. And seeing it, the Prince set his hands on the reins and checked the horses and cried aloud:

"What is this horror?"

So the charioteer, Channa, with fear tearing at his vitals, yet compelled by a force beyond all resistance to no other than the truth, answered:

"Prince, it is a sick man. The four elements are all confused and disordered, he is worn, feeble, and strengthless, tortured in body and mind, dependent upon the mercy of men whose own evil day is but postponed."

And a shudder ran through the crowd as the Prince questioned him, shrinking back as one in mortal fear.

"And this too is the common doom?"

"Prince, none escape it."

"And the few poor years that old age leaves us are broken into misery like this?"

"Prince, so it is."

And he said:

"Turn my chariot again, I will go no further. I have seen what I have seen."

So the news was carried to the Maharaja and he was almost beside himself, raging with anger that was half fear, and he sent for his wise minister, and cried to him:

"What shall we do? For my son is learning the

guarded secrets, and if I keep him shut in the gardens he will rebel and break away, and if I send him through the city such devils are my servants that horrible sights afflict him and disperse my hopes in him. Here have I built a Paradise so heavenly that could he but see it I need fear no more, for the man is not born who could leave its deep and delicious shades for the dusty world. And there have I placed a golden maiden whose smile is sunshine and her lips singing roses, and were he to see her— But what do I say? Is it not possible to a great person like myself that for a few short hours the city ways should be guarded from horror while he passes through? I am fallen indeed, otherwise."

But the old wise minister shook his head.

"Great sir, one should say it is possible, yet when I remember how the city was searched and guarded this twice, what dare I say? O Maharaj—may it not be that the high Gods being resolved may not be thwarted, and that we fight against iron destiny? Great fear possesses me."

But his master replied angrily:

"Foolish old man! And was I not given the choice? If I could withhold the truth he would be a great world-King. If he guessed it he would be an ascetic of the jungles. What father would choose other than I have done? Once more I will send him to my Paradise, and if this time I am tricked let your head answer it."

And again the Prince was sent out, but this time also though the city was decorated and garlanded there was no semblance of joy, and the very horses went with drooped heads as though fear were the charioteer.

And as they reached the street, where most the people crowded, the Divinity was again ready with his work, having prepared a sight terrible and woeful. For slowly preceding the chariot there went a funeral train, with four men bearing a bier and lying on it a body cold and stiff, with dropped jaw and dreadful dead eyes staring blindly at the sun. Withered flowers lay on the bier and the mourners beat their breasts and wept aloud, filling the air with wailing and lamentation.

And the Prince, closing his eyes to shut out the horror, and clenching his palms, said:

"What is this?"

And Channa, not daring to look in his face, answered very low: bowed under the weight of words he was compelled to utter.

"That is a dead man, all his powers of body destroyed, life departed, his heart without thought, his intellect dispersed. His spirit is fled, his body withered, stretched out like a dead log, taken from all who loved him. And mourning they carry him forth to burn and obliterate him, for they—even they—will have no more of his presence now become loathsome, but cast him from them utterly. And this is Death."

And into his clenched hands he murmured:

"Is this also the common lot?"

And the charioteer replied, with hidden face:

"Prince, so it is. He who begins his life must end it. And thus. For death may at any moment seize us and carry us away into darkness."

Then Siddhartha sank down in the chariot, his soul warring with his body, catching at the leaning-board for support, hiding his face from the light of day as the dead man was borne on before him, and wailing and lamentation filled the air.

And into his clenched hands he murmured:

"O terrible delusion of mortal men, who born in pain and utterly deluded are brought through grief and sickness and old age to this frightful end! Disperse the people. Turn back my chariot. The whole world is a lie. I have seen what I have seen."

So the people melted silently away in tears, as clouds

disperse in rain. For seeing the Prince's horror and amazement in learning the truth, for the first time they also sounded the deeps of their own misery, and life appeared to them a traitor, and in all the universe was no comfort.

But Channa the charioteer, not daring to return because of the Maharaja's strict command, drove onward to the Paradise, and the Prince crouching in the silks and gold with face hidden neither knew or cared.

So at last they came in among the green lawns and pleasant waters and deep-leaved trees, the last hope of the Maharaja, and slowly and painfully he dismounted.

Suddenly about the chariot, running and fluttering like doves came the lovely ones provided for pleasure, beautiful as flowers in a Paradise of Gods, adorned with chains of pearls and other jewels.

Beautiful were they, each one chosen as merchants choose a pearl to complete a queen's necklace, for their eyes were long and languishing, half hidden in black lashes as stars in midnight, and their mouths pomegranate buds disclosing seeds of ivory, and down to the ankle rolled their lengths of perfumed hair.

Most beautiful is the bosom of a woman, for in its gentle curves are all love, all tenderness expressed, and these displayed its loveliness—dear as rare jasmine flowers, precious as sweet food to the hungry, unveiled or veiled as little in transparency like the running of shallow water.

And thus they surrounded him as he passed through the blossomed trees rapt in sorrowful meditation, pale with the terror of gazing for the first time on the face of Death.

So they fluttered about him, the lovely ones, skilled in all subtleties of love, shedding enticements as the moon distils dews of camphor. One, seeing him sad, saddened her sweet face and looked at him with tears hanging on long lashes, as though she would say—"Dear Prince, I, too, have tasted grief. Do I not know?" And one, smiles chasing one another to cover in her merry eyes, promised forgetfulness, gladness in her arms, and some, clinging together like sister roses on twined stems, seemed to defy severance even if love should call them, tempting him who watched them to essay that sweet sorrow.

But amidst them the Prince paced lost in grief, not seeing them, or, seeing, heeding not at all. And presently when they had tried all their arts and could draw his regards no more than remote stars can draw the gaze of a cold moon, they fell silent and gathered fearfully into groups,—drawing back.

Now there stood in the shade of the bamboos a man much about the person of the Maharaja, sent to see if all were well, and when the Prince passed on, careless, this nobleman, Udayi, came out and addressed the silent beauties.

"You women, all so graceful and fair, are you thus worsted? Surely in all ages men have been subject to women when they put forth their power. Too soon are you discouraged—too soon. For this Prince, though he restrains his heart with the bit and bridle of purity, is but a man, and the wisest and greatest in time past have slipped where they thought themselves secure. And there is no fetter strong as white arms about a man's neck. Strive after new devices. Redouble your efforts. Great is the prize."

And the maidens, ashamed and angry at his chiding, fluttered again about the Prince where he sat in the shade of a jambu tree, putting forth amorous enticements, forgetful of all modesty and womanly reserve, pressing on, striving to move him.

But he in his great heart, sorrowful, apart, looked upon them, sighing.

" O creatures most miserable, unheeding the dooms of age and death, forgetful of the briefness of beauty, unconscious that above your throats is suspended the sharp two-edged sword, how wretched is your empty playing in the very jaws of destruction ! "

And though he spoke nothing, they saw the homeless horror in his eyes, and again they shrank away afraid.

So seeing the Prince alone, Udayi, smooth of speech, came softly along the pleasure-paths of the Paradise, brushing aside the flowers, observant and quiet as a serpent, and saluting the Prince he drew up beside him and spoke this :

" Prince in whom all beauty and nobility meet, you sit here sad and alone, and it is therefore that your great father, consumed by care for your welfare, appointed me to act as beseems a friend. Permit me then to speak, for a wise friend removes what is unprofitable, promotes real gain, and in adversity is true."

And Siddhartha, lifting his eyes, said :

" Speak, if indeed in this great strait there be anything to say.

So, supporting his arm on a bough of the fire-flame tree, Udayi spoke, inclining his delicate dark face and subtle eyes toward the Prince.

" True it is that sickness may assail us and that old age and death will by no means be baulked of their prey, yet youth is youth and beauty divine, and the man who turns his back on pleasure because it passes is a coward. Indeed the rose is the sweeter because even in blooming it treads the way of death and soon we see it no more. Truly, my Prince, you are afflicted with a distempered mind. Acquiescence is the secret of life. We who are wise know that these things must be, and even old age and death, the conquerors, we take to enhance our pleasures, saying to ourselves, " The moment is mine, and love is sweet and lust the spur of life. This moment neither death nor old age can take from me. I will spend it as a man would spend his all if he knew that next day he would be plundered, and a beggar."

But Siddhartha was silent, with brooding eyes fixed on the ground, and presently Udayi resumed, in a delicately modulated voice:

"While you believed that joy and beauty were eternal, and that ages hence these women would still surround you, beautiful and yielding, then you might well shrink from a delight too prolonged, for dropped honey cloys. An eternity of love may well become hell. Was it not so, my Prince."

And slowly the Prince answered:

"It was so. I have looked on the racing river, swollen with melting snows, thinking that, were any end possible, to be hurled beaten and broken down the rocks in its mad hurry were better than the changeless Paradise of love and soft words and swooning music. There you are right, Udayi the smooth-tongued. This is true."

And highly satisfied, Udayi resumed:

"And now, having learnt that there *is* an end, what should be your course? The pleasures of a prisoner released, who enjoys knowing that he has a respite though the doors will shut upon him one day. Surely it is not the part of a brave man to fling away what he has because he cannot have all, nor to own himself conquered because one day he must face the enemy whom as yet he has not seen. No—not so. Take what the Gods send—the Gods who have themselves been amenable to beauty and docile in the arms of loveliness. Indeed, what choice is there but to slink through life starting at every shadow, or to dice and drink and love, like a man tasting the best while it lasts. For what comes after we cannot tell. Who knows?"

And the Prince said:

"This has the sound of wisdom, yet wisdom it is not. There is an answer—there is a way, but I have found not it. It may be that it cannot be found—that there is no such thing. Yet, better the search than dully to agree with necessity. And as for these women— To me they are no enticement, and if I would I cannot. Under their fair faces I see the skull and they mop and mow likes apes in the face of Horror. If the Gods have thus made the world it is a folly and a brutality and they are more foolish than men who must abide their cruelties, and if they have not made it and all is chance we sink in the slough lit only by the flicker of dying dreams. Leave me, Udayi the smooth-tongued. I would be alone."

And the courtier crept silently away under green shades, treading lightly on turf and blossoms, thanking destiny that he was not as Siddhartha but could lift the brimming cup and drain it to the dregs, savouring every sparkle. And in his heart he mocked him, laughing at his weakness—he whose name is now remembered only because one day he spread out his folly before the Perfect One!

But the Prince, bending his great brows upon life and death, sat beneath the jambu tree, feet folded, hands laid upon his knees in perfect immobility. And he thought:

"Hollow compliance and a protesting heart! Is this life? Is there a better? Great are the concerns of life and death. So great, so awful that the poor race of mankind struggles only to forget for a brief moment what it can never comprehend. For all about us are seen injustices that were a King to commit his miserable people would rise and hurl him from his bloody throne. And we are told by the priests that the Gods have committed these crimes and yet are worthy of worship and honour. No—rather is it the propitiation of fiends who will torture us if they have not the servility of our praises while we die for their pleasure. And the good suffer and the evil flourish, and to the rich man is given more riches and to the poor more toil even exceeding their strength. Now indeed all that was hidden from me bursts upon my mind as when a flash of lightning tears the dark, and things I put aside for want of comprehension shriek aloud in my ears. Why am I clothed in jewels, why is my father generous and good, and my wife the fairest and most loving of women, when at this moment were my eyes opened they would behold men dying for bread that the least of my jewels would buy, with none to tend or pity them. And why are my deserts more than theirs? And why are some evil and some good as it were by nature? O cruel Gods who, lapped in far-off pleasures, care nothing for our agonies and let fall your good things on the wicked and evil things on the good—yourselves perhaps the sport of chance, if indeed you are at all!"

And these thoughts and many like them, black and miserable, stormed about him in the wreckage of the world.

And at long last he aroused himself and the Paradise was empty of all but a broad moonlight that lay in glories of light and shadow on trees and waters and there was deep silence. For the women, ashamed and terrified, had slipped noiselessly away and so back to the city, and far off down a long glade his chariot and wearied horses stood waiting in marble patience, and Channa sat beside them, his head bowed upon his raised knees like an embodied grief.

Very slowly the horses paced through the city, and that also was empty of all but moonlight, for not a living soul went or came in the quiet, and the pacing of the horses echoed loudly down the empty ways.

And not a word was spoken as they went, but when

they reached the House of the Garden, a woman ran out to meet them veiled like a ghost in the moonlight, and cried aloud:

" O happy Prince, and happiest,—the Gods are good to this glad House and to you, for on the bosom of the Princess lies your first-born son."

And at these words a strange trembling seized him, so that for a moment he hid his face in his hands. Then pale in the moonlight he said these words:

" A fetter, a fetter is set upon me, therefore call the child Rahula, a Fetter."

## CHAPTER VI

Now at the birth of her son, so great was the joy of the Princess that life and death were little things in her eyes, black rocks submerged in bright water glittering with sunshine, and every day she blossomed more beautiful and the child in her arms was like the star shining within the moon's crescent. And seeing this, what could the nobility of Siddhartha do otherwise than hide his grief and deep searchings of a heart tossed like waves in a mighty wind.

Beautiful in his eyes was the tenderness of the lovely mother and her eyes dwelling upon him and the child, but terrible also, remembering that at any moment the bright picture of life might break asunder and disclose beneath the lurking horror of death and the dark and unknown hereafter.

For if the Gods with their utmost forethought had made the world so full of shameful things, what wise man could trust such unskilful workmen for the world to come, and no hope was left anywhere.

He sat much alone by Rohini, his gaze dwelling on the silver peaks far off and serene in blue air, and at his feet little fish darted in the transparency of the pure waters, and the pheasant would lead her brood to his unmoving feet, and the shimmering peacocks feed beside him. And when the wild white swans spread snowy vans above his head, taking wing for the mountains and for far lands beyond that he knew not, it seemed in his deep musings that all these happy creatures were subject to a law they knew and obeyed with content and that their life was better than his own.

But compassion grew daily in his heart now that his eyes were opened—Compassion for all the sorrows that surrounded him bleeding in his heart like a wound such as drains life itself away. He saw the little lovely dancer Amra drag wearied feet through the dance one night and called her to him.

"Child, what ails you?"

"Great my lord, I must not tell you. But I dance no more. To-morrow I go."

"Child, I command you to speak. What is it?"

She looked about her with eyes large and fearful as the deer's when she sees the hunter's knife glitter above her.

"Great my lord, it is an order. I dare not speak."

"My order stands higher. Speak."

She trembled as she stood, with fear and weakness.

"My lord, it is the sickness. Two years ago my sister Vijaya was a dancer. Yourself has commended her. But the cruel cough came and tore her breast, and at last she could scarcely lift her little feet, and then they sent her secretly away, and she spat blood and the cough devoured her, and she died. And now it has taken me also and the blood came from my mouth last night, and to-morrow I go. But O I beseech your greatness to hide my words, for it is forbidden that any grief should soil the air about your noble presence."

"But when you rest, the cough will decline and you will be glad again, my sister."

"Great Prince, I shall die. For this there is no cure."

There was a long silence.

"And do you fear this?"

"My lord, I fear very terribly—but there is no help. What must be, must. And I am now too weary to dance, and it is better I die for I am a burden and a distress to my mother now I am worth no more money, and she is poor. There is scarce bread to eat."

Then the blood poured into the pale face of Siddhartha for shame and horror, and he said:

"On such foundations was my happiness built, and others have bled and wept that I might laugh! O, evil Gods, shameful and disastrous to man, if this is all! How shall the heart of man forgive your crimes against us, and where is justice in all the wide Three Worlds?"

And as he spoke he lifted the chain of pearls from his shoulders and threw them upon the dancer's, and she, beholding his nobleness and grief with tears, went sobbing away.

The next day he sent a message to the Maharaja.

"Great father, since now I know all the secrets and there is nothing hidden from me of the world's woe, what hinders that I should go free to see it? It may be that some joy shall meet my eyes and relieve the burning of the flame of pity that consumes me. Also, since I have a son it is now surely well that I should see and know the lives of the people whom he and I one day shall rule. And I say this for truth, I am weary, weary even to death of the music and dancing and the miserable diversions of my prison, and if there be any hope for me it is in the things of men, for I have done with those of women and children. Set your prisoner free. It is your son who beseeches."

And when the Maharaja agreed, the Prince sent another message.

"And let the city be neither decorated nor feasting. I desire to see the life of the people as they live it, not as they would pretend it is lived to please us great ones."

And this too was conceded, but the Maharaja commanded that the chief minister and a guard of the Sakya lords should accompany the Prince.

Therefore once more the chariot and well-paced horses

were prepared, adorned with precious stones and gold glittering like splendid sunshine, and he passed through the city and out by the further gate into a new world hitherto unknown.

And as he went on, the road was smooth and white, and gardens gay on either side and trees loaded, some with flowers and some with fruit, and seeing this and knowing it unprepared for his eyes, his heart stirred under the snow of grief and thawed a little from its ice, for it seemed that the people who lived therein must know some happiness and freedom from misery. But as he went further the heat of the day strengthened and became like a weight of lead, oppressive even beneath the silken canopy of the chariot, and the sweat stood on his brow and his garments clung to the moisture of his skin and weariness weighed upon him.

But for all this the toil about him could not cease, for men must eat, and work be completed and the fields of the Maharaja ploughed, and he saw how the labourers struggled with painful exertion, their bodies bent, their wet hair falling about haggard faces, their bodies fouled with mud and dust. And some were old and some were weak, and yet all must greatly toil, and very pitiful was it to see their strained muscles and starting eyes.

The ploughing oxen also—they, toiling so pitifully and with no reward,—their lolling tongues and gaping jaws, the whip and goad indenting smooth flanks until bright blood-drops started and they trembled and shrank—all these things tortured the mind of Siddhartha as he sat silently observant. And he said within himself:

"The world is built on pain and its foundations laid in agony. O Gods, most cruel and unjust, if there be a way, where is it? If there be a Law of Peace, where shall I find it? For I am bound in the dungeons of despair."

And, nobly moved to sympathy, he dismounted from the chariot, forcing himself to look steadfastly upon the sufferings of man and beast, and he sat down beneath a jambu tree, reflecting on the ways of death and birth. And he desired his companions, the Sakya lords, to leave him and wander where they would, and they went away laughing with each other and talking, costly umbrellas borne over them in the heat until they should reach the shade of the forest and there rest beside their wines and fruits. And then, as was now his wont, he gave himself to deep meditation on life and death, on transiency, and the progress of all to decay, desiring with all his soul that somewhere, anywhere, he might behold the Changeless, the Abiding, and in that find rest. And he asked of his soul:

" Is there safety in riches ? Are the rich exempt and high in the Gods' favour. No—no, indeed,—for their very luxuries consume them body and soul, making their bodies the home of disease and death, and their souls the harbourage of cowardice and terror. For it is harder to leave a Palace of gold than a mud hovel, and these are the spoilt children of the universe. There is no refuge in riches. In all the Three Worlds I see no refuge at all from the three Enemies—death, old age, and disease."

And as he meditated, his heart thus fixed, the five senses, as it were, extinguished, lost in the clear light of insight he entered on the first stage of pure rapture. All low desires submerged and in an ecstasy that was not joy but perfect clarity he saw the misery and sorrow of the world, sounding its deeps of agony and loss, the ruin wrought by age, disease, and death,—the hopeless dark beyond.

Hitherto he had known only in part, but now the whole, even as an eagle suspended on unmoving pinions, floating in supernal sunshine looks down beholding the earth spread like a picture below him, and nothing hidden.

And suddenly a great light shone within him—not to be described in words nor in thought comprehended. And he said these words, radiant with the first dawning beams of illumination :

"I have heard the wisdom of men and it is the crackling of dry wood in a destroying fire. Now will I seek a Noble Law they have not known, a Law hidden and divine, and I will wrestle with disease and age and death and bind their terrors. For behind these things is Peace, if the way is opened. And I will seek until I die."

And slowly at length, passing downward from ecstasy his thoughts collecting centred again about things earthly, and he became aware that a man approached him, carrying a bowl in his hand, wearing a coarse robe of yellow, pacing slowly in the roadway. And their eyes met.

And it appeared to the Prince that he had never before seen a man who resembled this strange mendicant, and he rose to greet him with courtesy, saying in his heart :

"Who is this person ? For his face is calm and joyful, and his eyes bespeak a soul at rest. Nor has he the mien of one tricked by sensual happiness, but austerity and contentment guide him, and though he treads on earth it does not hold him. And what is this bowl in his hand ? I will accost him."

And this done, the stranger, with due salutation grave and wise, replied :

"Great lord, I am a religious mendicant, who, shuddering at the victorious onslaught of age, disease and death, seeing that all things are transient and permanence nowhere to be found, have left the fetters of my home behind me that I may search for some happiness that is trustworthy, that decays not, that is imperishable, that looks with equal mind on friend and enemy, and is regardless of wealth and beauty. Such is the only happiness that will content me."

And Siddhartha, in deep amazement on hearing thoughts thus resembling his own, inquired eagerly:

"And where, O wise man, do you seek it?"

"Great lord, I seek it in solitude, in the tranquillity of deep woods, free from molestation. There in the Quiet dwells enlightenment. And I carry this bowl that the charitable may deposit an alms of food within it, and this is all I ask of the world. And now, pardon haste, for my way lies onward to the mountains where the true light awaits me, and joy for its attendant."

And he passed onward and was no more seen, and it is related that this ascetic was that divinity veiled in flesh who had made known to the Prince the Three Terrors,—but this I cannot tell.

Be he what he might, this man left behind him the first hope that had enlightened the midnight of grief. And the Prince said within his soul:

"This too is a seeker, and this is the life I covet, for the pleasures of earth are but sea-waters enraging the thirst they seem to quench, and what now has life to offer but the search for truth? Were there no others in the world but my son, my father, my wife, then surely is it incumbent upon me to find some means for their deliverance, but since the whole wide earth weeps uncomforted, what a craven should I be, if I spared to help it even with my blood and tears for unguents to its wounds. The way most surely opens before me, and the cry of the conquering ages is in my ears."

And after a time the Sakya lords, weary of their enjoyments, gathered about him and the horses were harnessed, and all returned to the city. And the people, rejoicing to see their Prince, gathered to meet and greet him, and one fair lady, leaning from a window, rejoicing in his beauty cried aloud:

"Happy is the father, happy the mother, happy the wife of such a son and husband."

But this word "happy" means also "freed," for are not freedom and happiness one? And taking her auspicious words for the cry of freedom he looked up smiling into her eyes, and said "Good is the teacher. Let this be her fee," unclasped his necklace of pearls and sent it to the happy lady and passed on, forgetting, while she dreamed in vain of love.

And all dispersed to their abodes.

But the next day the Prince entered into his father's presence, his face bright with resolution like the full moon, his step strong and steady as the gait of the King of Lions, noble and beautiful in strength.

And making due obeisance he asked:

"Is the Maharaj well and happy?"

"Well, my son, and rejoicing to see your face so bright and calm after long sorrow. Is the cloud past?"

"My father, it is past in part. A clear way lies before me."

"That, too, is well, Praise to the Wielder of the thunder and to all great Gods who hear our prayers."

Then tenderly, but with a calm immovable, the Prince declared his heart's desire.

"O kind father, worthy of all obedience, hear my case. The grief that has moved me is not my grief alone. Were I to die, I can die silent, after the manner of our race. But a man, when he beholds other men old, diseased, dying, is hurt, ashamed, revolted that such things should be, and no way of conquering such evils. There is a way if it could but be found."

And the Maharaja replied with anger.

"What way? This is child's folly. These things have been from Eternity, and men have faced the common lot as best they could, taking their pleasure where they might. What would you have more than others? Life is good, if you will but see it."

But Siddhartha answered steadfastly.

"O my father, I desire your august permission to seek the solitude, and there, deeply meditating, to find true deliverance not only for myself but for you and all the world."

And when the Maharaja heard these words—"to seek the solitude" a great trembling of the heart seized him, and his strong voice choked in his throat. And at last, even as the mighty wild elephant shakes with his weight the boughs of a fair green sapling in the jungle, he caught the hands of the Prince and clung to them most pitifully, crying aloud:

"Stop. Let not such ill-omened words be spoken. The time is not yet come—even if come it must. You are young and full of life and your heart beats to a glad measure. If you were to do this miserable thing you would bitterly repent it. You have not the strength, nor the knowledge. This is a resolution for old men, world-wearied. But you—beautiful as the day, full of youth, husband of a fair and dutiful wife, father of a young son, what talk is this? My son, I am ashamed for you. It is for me to undertake the ascetic's life, for you to rule in Kapila. Let it be so, and I will go."

And Siddhartha, holding his father's hands tenderly replied thus:

"My father, honoured and loved, you are the ruler and what have I to do with putting you from your seat? No—far be it from me! Rule in gladness and honour until the appointed day. But for myself—there is but one condition on which I can stay! If you will assure me against old age, disease, and death, I will remain--but not otherwise."

And the Maharaja, blind with grief, the white hairs showing on head and beard, said only:

"Such words are impious. Am I a God that I can say to these three, 'Thus far and no farther?' No—Betake yourself to pleasure and business like other men and forget. There is no other remedy."

But Siddhartha flung himself on his knees before his father and grasped his robe in the agony of his pleading.

"Father, hinder me no more if you love me. If I were shut in a burning house would you bar the door? Let me solve my doubt for it consumes my very life. O let me go, let me go! For if not—what way is left? Men have slain themselves for a lesser hope than mine, that perhaps down the dark ways of death they might seek and find what they could not in this world of lies and counterfeits."

But he appealed in vain for the ears of his father were sealed, and when after pleading even to anguish the Prince had left him grave and silent, he issued orders that the Garden House should be guarded more strictly than before—that fresh dancers, fresh music, should be ordered and new pleasures invented and that every road and way should be watched with ten-fold diligence.

And Siddhartha seeing the tears of his father with a compassion that pierced his own heart returned to the Garden House, and set himself in silence to consider, not knowing whence help would find him, but firm in his resolve.

And beneath the trees Yashodara awaited him, carrying his young son in her arms, and she knelt beside him, uncovering the face of the child, bright and beautiful as a budding rose in earliest summer. For she thought—"Let this plead for me," and Siddhartha read the little face so like his own, in silence.

Then, stretching out his hand, he clasped the hand of his wife, and spoke thus:

"Well-beloved, if our child were in a house ruining

about him, and I stood by to see him crushed and broken, what would be your thoughts of me?"

She smiled with pride and contentment.

"Why ask? That could not be. You would give your life for him and count it nothing."

"Well-beloved, mother of my son, that word is true; you know it. And would you who love me hold me back if I rushed on death for his sake, counting my own life as nothing?"

"For my love's sake I would bid you go."

"True again. So speak, so do the women of our race. But hear further. Suppose my son fallen into bitter poverty, and that I knew of a great treasure hidden in far-off forests and mountains, so far that great was the danger, great the severance, would you bid me stay or go?"

Doubt clouded the beauty of her eyes raised toward him.

"There, my heart's lord, I know not. You are more to my son and me than any treasure. What are jewels, pearls or gold compared with the heaven of your presence? Better poverty together and the blue heaven above us and bright earth beneath, than loneliness and splendour."

Clasping her hand he answered:

"But starving, his face gaunt with want, haunted by ghosts of grief and fear, would you send me or bid me stay? Think well, mother of my son. Would you weigh your grief against his good, and he too young to know?"

And she answered:

"I would say, Go—how otherwise? But, O beloved, these words are dreadful. Forget them. Look at the sunset strewing roses on the cold snows and the splendour of Surya driving his chariot down the western sky after the long day of glory. He is weary of pomp and colour.

He longs for the cool refreshing dews and the dusk and quiet and the dark repose of midnight. Would that we could see him face to face, golden-eyed and inconceivably divine. The Gods are far and grief is near."

He loosed her hand gently.

"Those words are true also, wise and beautiful." And slowly he added;

"Night comes and the Gods are far. Go in and sleep, beloved,—Yet do not forget the words we have spoken together, for grief comes to all and when it comes there is but one way—to agree nobly with necessity."

And she took the dust from his feet, rapt on the beauty of his eyes and went, carrying the child with her.

# Part II

# CHAPTER VII

THUS have I heard:

On that night of terror and wonder were strange influences astir in the darkness, influences moving steadily to war. For the battle was not between the armies of Kings nor was the prize a throne, but a combat strange, unearthly between the armies of the Appetites and Desires, and the warriors of the World of pure spirit and wisdom eternal, and there and thus was it fought.

It was the night of No Moon and the stars hung larger and brighter, suspended but a little above the earth, and the dark was still and breathless, so that Siddhartha would have willingly sat all night by Rohini listening to the cool ripple of water as she made her way through the gardens to an end he knew not. But this could not be, for by the Maharaja's new orders the women must dog his footsteps, never permitting him to wander, or remain unseen. And thus, though they were invisible, he knew that bright eyes watched in every brake, and feet light as a spirit's trod noiselessly where he went.

Therefore at last, sighing, he rose and passed into the Hall where the dancers stood ready to sway in their beautiful measure, and the singers and musicians were ranged in order, fair face outshining fair face until the most beautiful were nearest to the gold cushions of his seat. But the Princess Yashodara slept far off in the little marble chamber with her child clasped to her bosom.

And at last as the night went on a deep weariness

oppressed him and lay like lead on his eyelids, and the subtly stealing dark and wearisome iteration of music and of rhythmic feet became like an opiate, and his head dropped on the raised pillows and he slept. So the dance slackened quietly and the dancers whispered one to another:

"How pale is the Prince! How careworn! Was it wise in the Maharaj to hide from him what cannot be hidden? But we are dancers—this is not our business. Do not wake him lest there be anger. Mute the instruments very slowly and softly and let none jangle as we lay it aside. We must not leave him alone, lest suddenly he awake and demand more pleasure, therefore remain here but be very quiet and, if it be possible, sleep. O, it is good to rest. We, too, are weary of singing and dancing. It is a hard service. Sleep, sisters, sleep."

And it is told that when midnight drew veils of darkness over earth and sky there came Influences noiseless—winged as the white moth that haunts the evenings of summer, and that as these came, thought died from the soul of Siddhartha and it became Perception,—and he saw and heard inwardly while the women about him lay drunk with heavy sleep.

Now along the night crept a strange music, thin at first and faint as the far-off falling of rain, but drawing nearer, nearer, sweeter than all harps and lutes struck with earthly hands, and at first no words could be distinguished but only an unearthly sweetness, soul-dividing, purer than the crystal purity of ice on the highest summits of the mountains that speak face to face with heaven.

And at last the clear sounds glided into clear words, and the Prince heard the mystic music, whether within or without his soul who shall say? But it fell from on high like white flakes of snow falling cold and passionless and drowning desire.

"Mighty One, O Mighty One.
There is a Way—a Way.
The wise of old have trodden it.
Rise now and go.
Finding the Light,
Share it with men.
Grant unto all
To drink in peace
The water of Righteousness.
Thou who in past lives
Didst agonise for men,
Nothing withholding,
Again go forth,
Conqueror of sorrow."

And as he listened in tranced silence once more the clear words shaped themselves from the heart of silence.

"Light of the world,
Remember past lives.
Griefs without end,
Revilings and prisons,
Deaths many and cruel.
These hast Thou borne,
Loving and patiently,
Shedding forgiveness
On those who slew thee.
Go forth again,
Riding to Victory."

And when he heard and had understood this music, the Prince rose from sleep and looked about him in the faint light of the lamps, with thoughts new and awful stirring in his breast—thoughts beyond words, unutterable.

And the women slept in disorder about him, heavily

lolling as though drunk with wine, their faces wried and twisted, mouths awry, running over with saliva, limbs flung into coarse attitudes, sprawling, couchant like animals, with pendent lips and breasts, laughing foolishly at worthless dreams, hidden blemishes visible, abandoned to the disclosures of careless sleep, ungainly, revolting, as though the truth had suddenly touched them with clear ray disclosing them as they were.

And the Prince said slowly:

"It is a graveyard, and these are the corpses."

And shrinking in his very soul, he rose, looking down upon them with horror, and drawing his feet and garments from the contact went forth treading quietly and ascended to the roof of the House of the Garden to look out into the night.

Dead silent was it as he turned to the eastern horizon, the air breathless as though the Universe waited in suspense to know what he would do.

But he, standing alone in the night, joined the ten fingers of his hands, and rendered homage to all the Enlightened who had preceded him, exalting and uniting his purpose to theirs who had opened the way which the eternities shall not close.

And even as he joined his hands he perceived that the bright star Pushya which had shone upon his birth was rising in the sky, and he knew that his hour was upon him.

Then, turning, he descended, led by human anguish and longing to see once more his young child and its mother, for in the very deeps of his heart those lives were rooted, but, lest resolution should waver, he went first to the doorway where slept Channa the charioteer, wrapped in his white garment, and even as the Prince stooped above him, this man sprang to his feet, alert and faithful, saluting his Prince,—and in dim lamplight each looked into the eyes of the other.

And Siddhartha said:

"O faithful! The blessing that is upon me has this night touched perfection. Bring out my noble white horse, for my life here is done and I depart."

But Channa stood perfectly silent staring in his face as one bereft of purpose, and once more Siddhartha spoke.

"What must be, must. I thirst and long for a draught of the Fountain of Sweet Dew. Delay no more. Saddle white Kantaka. It is an order."

And Channa obeyed.

So the Prince entered the little marble chamber where on her golden bed lay the Princess, drowned in sweet sleep, clasping the child in her arms, unconscious of the grief approaching. And it appeared to Siddhartha that the cold air of his sorrow must rouse her, but it did not. She slept and smiled, rapt in a dream of content. And garlands of flowers hung about the chamber mingling their perfumes with the pure air of night breathed through marble lattices, and all this was home and his, and for the last time he looked upon it. And so great a desolation fell upon him that twice he stretched his empty arms to clasp the child in all its rosy warmth and dearness, and twice they fell because he feared to wake Yashodara from her last dream of joy.

So he stood, enduring, looking upon them as a man who faces death, and for a while he stayed, with thoughts that cannot be told, nor should that veil be lifted.

But when the end was come and he could endure no more, he stooped above them until his breath mingled with theirs, and turned away leaving them sleeping.

Then, passing through the quiet house, he came to the doorway where stood white Kantaka, and Channa held him, pale as death.

Now this horse was of all most noble, high-maned, with flowing tail, broad-backed, wide-browed, with round and claw-shaped nostrils, and he stood regarding his lord, and there was prescience in his great eyes. And the Prince soothed and caressed the strong neck, saying:

"O brave in fight and fearless, now put forth strength in a sterner battle. To-night I ride far—even to the River of Eternal Life. I ride far to seek deliverance—not for men only, but for all your kind also. Therefore for your own sake, great horse,—for the sake of all that draw the breath of life, carry me far—far this night."

And so, springing upon the noble horse, he settled himself in the saddle, and pacing quietly the horse went on his way. So they passed out dreamlike, the man like the sun shining forth from his cloudy palaces, the horse like the white cloud beneath him, drawing quiet breath because no sound must awake the house of sleepers.

And it is told—but I know not—that four attendant divine spirits laid their hands beneath the strong ringing hoofs to deaden the sound, and that others, casting the watchmen into sleep, caused the heavy barred gates to roll open slowly and noiselessly. But be that as it will it is certain that the Prince passed out, and gaining the road before the gates, stopped and turned, saying these words:

"Never again shall I come here—never again see this beloved place, unless I conquer old age, disease, and death, for this is my quest."

And it is told that divine voices in the air cried aloud: "Well done. Well said." And whether the Prince heard this or no I cannot tell, but he rode on his way. And man and horse, strong of heart, went far that night, so far that when the east flashed into light and the world-wide radiance of the rising sun they stood beside great woods and the habitations of those ascetics who had relinquished the world.

There, wearied, the royal horse himself stopped, to draw restful breath and to drink the pure lymph of those crystalline streams. So the Prince dismounted and looking into the horse's eyes he said:

"You have borne me well." And from that he turned to Channa, saying:

"And you, O faithfullest, swift-footed as a bird is swift-winged, long have you followed me, and even before this night my heart was full of gratitude, and I knew you as a true man,—strong of heart and strong of body. But now I know more, for you have come with me utterly disdainful of profit, courting danger and rebuke, and what shall I say to you? Many words I cannot say—but only this. My heart will remember. But, here we part—here is our relationship ended. Take my horse and return. For me are births and deaths about to be ended."

And taking off the chain of beaten gold and glimmering jewels which he wore about his neck, he gave it to Channa, saying:

"Take this in remembrance. Let it console your grief."

Then loosing the precious jewel that shone in his head-tire, he looked at it lying in his palm where it flashed resplendent like the sun of Indra's Paradise, and he said slowly:

"Take this, Channa, to my father and lay it reverently before him. It is my heart. Tell him that I have entered upon the life of the ascetic, not indeed seeking a heavenly birth, for what is that to me if again I fall into rebirth and it leaves me in this world of lies and illusions?—but that I may find the Way of Deliverance. For if that way is found then no more need I leave those whom I love; no more put away my kindred. But since I must go, let not my father endure grief for me. Let him forget me and be glad."

Then Channa, listening with reverence, tried to make his voice heard, choking with grief.

"This will I do—but O the heaping up of sorrow! How shall it be endured? Your father increases in years, your son is but a little infant, the sister of your mother, who tended your childhood, loves you as a son,—your wife, the mother of your child— My Prince, my Prince!—think better before all are lost. And drive me not from you. If I have been faithful is not trust the reward of fidelity? O turn for pity's sake: set your face homeward. This I beseech you."

But the Prince, pale and resolved, made answer:

"What is relationship? Were I to die I must leave them. My own mother loved me, but she is vanished from among us. The kinships of this world are like a flock of birds that for a night settle on the same tree and when dawn comes disperse. Such are its ties, no more. Does any tie of relationship ensure the joy of permanent union? No. All is said. Say no more, faithful one. Return to the city and make known to all men these my words—'When I have found the Way—that Way which puts an end to the sad endless chain of birth and death, then and not otherwise I will return.' And if I do not obtain this victory my body shall perish in the jungle."

And as he turned to go, the horse, hearing, bent his head and licked the foot of the Prince, and grief was seen in his large eyes. So the Prince, fondly stroking his head, bade him also farewell.

"My horse, gentle and noble, your good deeds have gained their reward. No painful rebirth awaits you—this I know. Be content, for it is well."

Then, taking his jewelled sword, shining like a meteor, he cut off the knot of hair which as a Prince he wore twisted with jewels, and even as he did this there passed a hunter going toward the jungle with bow and arrows and wearing a garment of coarse yellow, and Siddhartha hailed the man.

" Friend, will you change your garment for mine, for with mine I have done for ever."

And the man drew near, consenting, and stripped off his garment and took the other, and for a moment the two looked each other in the eyes, Channa standing by.

Now it is told—but this I cannot know—that this hunter was the same divine spirit, who disguised in flesh had brought enlightenment to the Prince, but be that as it may, he took the garment and went his way in silence.

And having made this exchange Siddhartha took off his jewels one by one and placed them in the hands of Channa, and stood a moment in the dull garment as it were a bright star in eclipse, and so looked into the faithful eyes of Channa—as though he would have spoken. But this he could not then slowly turning he made his way to the forest, and its boughs and leaves opened to receive him, he parting them with his hands, and he passed in and was seen no more.

And Channa left alone, cried aloud.

" It is done."

Raising his hands to the unpitying skies and letting fall his arm on the neck of Kantaka, he stumbled homeward, his tears falling, and great fear and grief possessing his soul.

And here and thus ends the scripture of the great Renunciation leading us onward to the Discipline, the Enlightment and the Victory.

## CHAPTER VIII

THUS have I heard:

Going deeper into the forest, calm and resolved in mind, startling the deer as he passed, the birds rising about him with cries, the Prince went on his way, plucking the wild berries and fruits for food, he who had been served from gold and silver: and the sun now fully risen poured floods of light between the quivering leaves and ancient branches of those venerable trees. And as he passed, seeing the world so beautiful, dew trembling like crystals upon leaf and flower and the perfume of the morning exhaling like the breath of a maiden in pure mist, the beginning of peace rose in his troubled mind, and he said within himself.

" After a great storm comes calm. Let me now control my grief, remembering that the past returns no more than Rohini after she has flowed into the ocean. And as in the ocean drifting logs for awhile meet and touch and are then driven apart by the waves, so is it with parents, wives, children and wealth. This is most true."

And when at noon he was weary and his feet torn with the strong thorns and hooks of jungle creepers he sat down to rest and the thought came.

" Were I now in the sweet garden by Rohini how would my wife, soft-handed, gentle-voiced, weep to see these feet, with what cool dropping unguents would she staunch the blood, which now I have not so much as a rag to wipe away."——

So, seeing this and waiting his opportunity, Mara, the Tempter—that One evil from of old, drew near through the shining trees, and whether he spoke within or without the heart of Siddhartha I cannot tell, but most certainly he spoke, and his voice at first distant as the humming of ardent black bees about a flower became nearer, sweeter, subtle, until it sealed every sense to all but its meaning. And thus he said:

"O Prince, merciful and compassionate but utterly misled, what is it you would do in the wild forest? Is this a place for a ruler of men? Far be it from you! By what evil counsel do you abandon your duties, flinging all madly aside to become an ascetic? What reason is there in believing that pain and destruction of the body give wings to the soul? No—but far otherwise, for the soul dwindles with the tortured body as flame dies when it has consumed the fuel. And if your aim be to benefit mankind, are not just and powerful Kings needed, and was it not foretold at your auspicious birth that you would become an empire-ruling King? Here—living and dying in the jungle, how is your might wasted, and the people forsaken!"

And the voice grew sweeter and more poignant and verily before him did Siddhartha see the face of the Tempter, beautiful and melancholy with pleading mouth and eyes that entreated, and hands spread out in prayer.

"Think better, O Prince. Consider how the kingdom of Kosala lies near to Kapila and easily to be captured. Great are the cities of Kosala. Consider the city of Ayodhya—in length it is eighty-four miles, in breadth seventy, and the streets so broad that a team of elephants —nay two, might be easily driven abreast, and flowering trees stand along them, and there are rows of stalls to which the wealthy merchants flock from all the countries of the world, from China and Lanka and down the Passes from Balkh and Samarkhand; their caravans of camels and horses carrying such rarities as kingly hearts desire. There are gardens and mango groves for the delight of the citizens and clear waters where they may sport like swans and other aquatic birds, and mountain-like palaces adorned with pinnacles and banners and glittering with precious inlay,—and great houses where skilled actors delight their hearers with song and dance and story, so that eye and ear are transported in seeing and hearing. And there is a quarter of the city where dwell women of beauty exceeding the Apsaras, for they are brought from the ends of the earth to delight the happy people of Kosala. And the town is thronged with splendid elephants and horses; and neighbouring kings, decked with earrings and armlets, come to pay tribute, and marvel at the glittering beauty of the city. There is no want of food and the very water is sweet as the juice of the sugar-cane, and night and day the air resounds with music and stringed instruments. And all this is yours for the taking."

And heart-enthralling was the picture that rose before the Prince's eyes in hearing, for he beheld Yashodara a Queen beside him, fair and royal, example to women, and between his knees his son Rahula proud and gentle—a great King to be, and a happy people sheltered in his shadow—a noble people enlightening the dark tribes about them. And the soft voice proceeded like the breathing melody of a flute.

"Nor are the Gods forgotten in the city of Ayodhya; great reverence is done them, and were a royal saint upon the throne, crime would be banished and forgotten and the Golden Age return to earth. O bountiful and merciful, all this is in your hands. There also are troops of noble Brahmans, celebrated for learning and piety, for it were shame indeed if greatness of mind and soul were forgotten in the pleasure of the senses. No—far otherwise. And with such wisdom there is no poverty, for every householder is rich in horses and cattle and food. All possess earrings and garlands, each is content with his own gains, free from covetousness, speaking the truth."

And when the sweet subtle voice ceased, the Prince replied:

"Then it is only I who shall be covetous—I, who must plunge this happy city in blood and tears that I may take it to be my slave? And the King who has made them happy I must slay. Is this what you would have me do?"

And the Tempter replied gravely:

"Prince, there is no good but what it might be better, and if that King is wise you are wiser. Turn again to Kapila and to glory, and to the good of mankind, and this that I promise shall befall in seven days."

Then summoning his fortitude, Siddhartha said slowly:

"This city filled with pleasure, beauty and wealth, with wisdom and content,—is it safely protected, O wise one? Is it well fortified against attack?"

And eager was the voice of the Tempter.

"Well asked, O Prince, and wisely. It is fortified as never city in the world's history. About it goes a mighty wall where the King's chariots may drive abreast, and about that a moat wide and deep, and there is a host of warriors, each able to combat with a thousand. Never city so safe. Nor could even yourself conquer it did I not give you friends within the gates."

"Then is it certain that age, disease and death, those fell enemies, must needs stay outside? They cannot enter in this guarded city?" So said the Prince.

There was silence. And presently Siddhartha answering the subtle voice, said:

"Go from me, thou Ancient Evil! The snare is set too plain. For all their wealth this miserable people must suffer and decay and die like all the world and their riches are but a pang the more. Truly one day I may come to Ayodhya and as a conqueror bringing great riches in my hand for their good, but not thus—not thus!"

And in his heart the subtle voice was stilled and he rose and went on his way with bleeding feet. And as he went he said this to himself:

"Before the days when I considered the terrors of re-birth, old age, disease and death, I sought after such merchandise as the merchandise of Kosala, subject to all these lures. But now, seeing the danger, awake and alert, let me seek only after the things which have no part in these, even the supreme joy and security of the Peace."

But though he did not know it, that Tempter followed, for who is immune from his arts, and he thought, watching the serenity of the Prince:

"This time he has conquered, but sooner or later, even if riches fail, some hurtful or malicious thought will burn within him and then—then he is mine."

And from that hour he crept behind the Prince on the watch for sin, cleaving to him like a shadow which follows the object from which it falls.

So after long journeying he came to Rajagriha—name never to be forgotten because once the Light of the world sojourned there. And this was the capital of King Bimbisara, King of Maghada, and it lay very pleasantly in an eastern valley of holy Ganges, surrounded by the five mountains of the Vindhya range, and these are beautiful though but as foothills comparing them with those great ramparts of the Gods—the mountains beyond Kapila.

Now in these Vindhya mountains are caves in the lower hills, all grown about by trees, in the solitude yet not so far but what an ascetic may go to the city if needful, and in these caves certain learned and holy Brahmans had established themselves, and to each came disciples, counting this world as husks if they might rise to the heavens on strong wings of knowledge and belief.

Coming wearily through the forest, pale and worn with unused hardships, the Prince climbed upward to the caves shaded by great trees and in an excellent quiet, and at last before him he saw the mouth of a cave hung with vines and grown about by bushes in blossom, and before it sat a man clothed in a garment of red bark, and he was in the lotus posture to ward off evil, and the Prince seeing him thus meditating passed around him respectfully three times and took his seat in silence at a proper distance, waiting his pleasure.

So time went by, and the ascetic never stirred though his shadow shifted as the sun went on his golden journey westward, and Siddhartha meditated on the Way of Peace, wondering if the man before him had its key, and to him, too, the time was not long, and the cool shade bathed his wounded feet and refreshed them.

And at last the ascetic returned to earth and looked at him with visionary incurious eyes while the Prince waited respectfully, and finally he accosted Siddhartha, asking what had brought him hither, to whom the Prince dutifully replied, for a teacher is more even than a parent, being a spiritual and not a fleshly father, and he besought his instruction.

And having heard, the Brahman Alara considered awhile, and agreed that he should study the Vedas and Upanishads, those ancient holy scriptures, under his guidance and amid the families of holy persons, both men and women, who dwelt in the caves and woods each engaged in religious duties and pursuing the way to Heaven.

And the Prince with folded hands, said humbly:

"I am but a beginner, great sir; I do not know the rules of the religious life. Be pleased to grant me information."

And that twice-born Brahman of high lineage informed Siddhartha of the rules of the various teachers and of the fruits expected from their practices. He declared how some lived only on food proceeding from pure water, some subsisting on edible roots and tender twigs, others on fruits and flowers, some, like deer, eating grass and herbs, others again begging their food and giving it in charity, keeping only the crumbs and remnants for themselves.

Also he named those ascetics who torture the body in order to subdue it, those who let water drop continually on their heads—and many more, cunning in devising sufferings and cruel austerities, so that at the end of every life they may purchase birth in Heaven and taste divine tranquillities and pleasures before they are again launched into the dreary sea of mortal existence.

"And thus," he said, "are great joys attained, impossible to be described in words, delectable to the soul."

And the Prince heard with reverence, and the ascetics, men and women who dwelt in the woods and caves, seeing the beauty of his face and his serenity and courtesy, were moved with wonder and admiration, saying—"Who is this most beautiful young man, so calm and noble? Surely he has the appearance of a great Prince and can be no other. Well is it when such forsake the world's things for the things of the Gods."

And his master appointed a cave for his dwelling tapestried with nests of the wild black-bees, and dripped about in one part with golden honey, but because the holy men were friendly to all creatures and disturbed none of their combs but only ate a little of the dripped honey, the bees were friendly also and pleasant companions, their myriad voices soothing to meditation as the sounds of a great ocean far off.

Here dwelt Siddhartha, joining in the strong chanting of Vedic hymns and hearing the recital of the Vedas and Upanishads, for books were none—the memories of men carrying all knowledge, and he learnt these things with a swiftness almost incredible, because his heart was in it. And when food was needed, clad in his yellow garment he took his begging bowl, and went down to the city begging from house to house, for he considered thus :

" Full of hindrances is the household life ; the haunt of passion. Free as air is the homeless state." And all the luxuries of his former life seemed empty as a dream that flies at dawn. " Better is the alms of food I beg than the wines and fruits cooled in snow, the rich meats and costly of Kapila." So he said night and day, though at first his soul loathed the food.

Now one day when he went to the town of Giribaja to beg his food it so happened that the King of Maghada, Bimbisara, stood on the high terrace of his palace, looking down the street, and he saw the young ascetic coming slowly, holding his bowl in his hands and courteously accepting what was given. And there was that in the nobility of his person and evident signs of Aryan birth which arrested the eyes of the King and he said to those about him :

" Look upon this man, lords, beautiful is he, great and pure. He is guarded in conduct ; his eyes do not wander ; he looks not more than a fathom's length before him. Such a man is of no low caste. See how, like a great noble, he is self-possessed and serene, moving in solitary majesty as the moon among faint stars. Send my royal messengers and inquire where that mendicant goes."

And the messengers ran at the King's word and hurried down into the street saying to one another.

"Where is that Bhikkhu[1] going? It is toward the mountain Pandava. That must be his abode."

And having followed where Siddhartha went they returned to the King and told him—

"On the eastern slope of Mount Pandava that Bhikku has taken his seat, a King among men as the tiger among beasts."

And the King said, "Bring out my chariot," and he directed it to the mouutain.

Now when the road ended he did not return discouraged, but dismounting went onward climbing up on foot until he came near to where the Prince sat, and there with eagerness and courtesy the King greeted him, for as lions know their kind, not mistaking them for jackals, so it is with the great. And the King took his seat on a rock, saying:

"I beseech you, sir, to tell me your family and lineage. Young are you, a man in his first youth, fine and delicate in colour, the glory of the vanguard of an army. I would lay wealth at your feet, if wealth delighted you. Speak, and tell me your mind."

And as he spoke the nobles stood grouped about to hear, correcting every careless or unseemly gesture because the man was great and the very air about him pure, and they beheld with joy his noble body bright as gold, his eyes of darkest blue, and the kingliness of his manners.

And the Prince replied with gratitude and noble courtesy:

"Great King, kind and liberal is your heart, and precious your generosity to my own, but all these things lie behind me far as dawn from sunset. I had wealth

[1] Monk.

and power, and more, but regarding these things as hindrances to perception I am come out into the solitude to seek the Way of Peace."

And having thus begun he related to the King his family and history, and all about them held breath to listen.

And the King, sighing, at last said this:

"Noble one, I cannot but reverence your choice yet I lament it, for the world has need of you. I would share my kingdom with you could that shake your resolution. There is nothing I could refuse would it draw you to us again for I see you surpassing other men and have not known your like."

But the steadfast Prince replied:

"Illustrious and world-renowned, descendant of Arya, your words are heard with deep veneration. Righteous and sincere, you speak the truth, and virtue is not confined to any one school of thought—the sun lights the whole world and the Way of a great and just King is blessed. But for me, I have heard a call. My way is onward and behind me lie the Five Desires. Would a hare rescued from a serpent's jaws go back to be devoured? As little would I return to the dreams and illusions that have fallen from me. King, there are many quests and mine is to find deliverance for the world from the Wheel of Agony that turns and turns and will not cease through pitiless ages of rebirth and sorrow. There is a way,—and I have given all that I may find it. But you—return, O wise King, to your happy city. May you direct and defend your subjects in peace. May the Gods be good to you. May all good go with you."

And the King replied with gratitude and noble courtesy: saying these words:

"That which you seek, great Prince, may you attain, receiving the perfect fruit of your birth. And when this is gained I pray you return to me that I also may share in your wisdom, and graciously receive me as one who would learn."

So the Prince rising, with courteous salutations, pursued his way to the solitude, and the King and his nobles with folded hands followed a little way in reverence and then with thoughtful and mindful hearts returned to the city.

## CHAPTER IX

THUS have I heard:

So while the Prince went on into the woods, turning his steadfast face to the dawn of Enlightenment, Channa the charioteer went slowly back to Kapila, grieving and weeping, leading the noble horse, for he had most surely hoped that where his lord went he might follow, having proved himself faithful; and as the darkness of night closed in upon him he wavered, halting and looking behind him and then again proceeding, irresolute in mind.

And the horse also grieved for his master, going heavily, his head bowed that was held so nobly, neither would he eat grass nor drink water, and no joy nor spirit were left in him, for he thought, "I shall never see him again." And even as he thought this, his great heart broke for grief, and he died. But in a happy place was he reborn because of his fidelity, even as the Prince had foreseen, for in no world can love lose the blessedness of its loving.

But Channa went yet more slowly, weeping a second sorrow, and to him the land appeared withered as when a man returns to a ruined city which once he knew glad and living, and it seemed as though the sun hidden behind a mountain no longer enlightened the world.

So the men about the way, seeing him in grief, turned again to look, and consternation seized them and one cried aloud:

"Where is the Prince—beloved of the world? Have

you taken him away by stealth? Where is he hidden?"

And Channa halting, said with sighs;

"I who followed him always with a loving heart, would I have left him? Little do you know me! He has dismissed me,—O men of Kapila! He has buried himself in the forests to live the life of an ascetic."

And those who listened heard this with dark foreboding, for it appeared to them that things deep, strange, and mysterious had suddenly appeared in their way and that the very world had changed in its course if such things could be. What had there been lacking to the Prince that he should go out thus to seek it? What had he beheld, invisible to them?

And the news spread from them to the city and men and women rushed out to the gates, and when they saw that Channa wept as he returned in loneliness, they, not understanding whether the Prince was dead or alive, cried out:

"What has befallen? Surely sorrow is added to sorrow."

And like the flash of lightning news spread to the House of the Garden, and the women of the palace, their hair dishevelled about them, their robes flung hastily on as for a night-alarm, came pouring down to the doors that they might hear the worst, and when they saw the charioteer alone, they raised a loud and bitter cry. So women mourn the beloved dead when hope itself is dead with him.

And the cry reached Prajapati, aunt and foster-mother of the Prince, sister of Maya his mother, and she wept, saying to herself.

"Alas—his beauty, his beauty! O my son, who was there to compare with him? I see his dark locks bound with gold, his eyes blue and deep as the Ox-King's, his broad shoulders and strong arms, a Tiger-King among men. How can it be endured that you should suffer the chills and heats of the forest and we, bereft and miserable, see you no more!"

And the great lady threw herself upon the earth and so lay, with the women sitting about her, held motionless by strong grief, as marble images.

And when at last one gathered up courage to tell the Princess, she sent for Channa, towering in indignation above him like an angry Queen.

"O faithless man, and trusted in vain! evil contriver, false servant!—beneath these pretended tears there is a hidden smile. You went out with him and alone you return. What have you done? Better an open enemy than a false friend. Alas, the sorrows of our line! Surely his noble mother died foreseeing the grief of to-day, for our house is left unto us desolate!"

And Channa, pierced to the soul and thunderstruck, was silent, and she spoke again.

"You weep aloud now. Why did you not awake the Palace when he went? Then all might have been saved. Now it is too late."

So, folding his hands, with no anger in his heart, for the agony of the Princess was visible, the true Channa replied:

"Great Lady, have pity on my grief, for I am innocent in this. In my soul I believe it was the Gods' doing. From the day of his birth there have been portents, and who was I to stand against it?"

Then the Princess, just and noble of soul, recollected herself, regretting her words, knowing well that the burden of the Gods' purpose is their own and cannot be charged upon a man, and she spoke gently to him, and when he was gone she sat alone mourning, recalling the face and voice of her Prince, and slowly as the strong grief overburdened her she slipped down strengthless from the golden cushions and lay upon the ground, her empty arms stretched out before her.

So her women found her, and as they raised her tenderly, she said this only:

"Take away my golden bed where my lord and I lay, for henceforth I will lie upon bare earth. Take away my robes of silk and my jewels and bring me the yellow robe of the mendicant, for I am beggared indeed. Henceforth I will wear no other. Cut off my long hair, for I have done with beauty. And once a day, and once only, bring me the food of the mendicant, such as will keep the flame of life alight and no more, for as to pleasure, the name of it is forgotten."

And as she said so was it done, and the long and perfumed tresses that touched her lovely feet fell about her like a dropped veil, and thus she lived henceforward, and for her child's sake only.

But as to the Maharaja his case was different, for love and anger contended in him, and his thoughts charged each other as in battle, rushing madly hither and thither like a herd of wild elephants. And when his nobles gathered about him he raged aloud before them:

"Once I had a son. Now I have none. What is my kingdom to me, and my horribly echoing empty palace? And what are rule and dominance? Why was he given to be taken?"

And for all the royal priest and the wise minister could do, they could not assuage his wrath and grief until the thought occurred to them that they might follow the wanderer and yet compel or persuade him to return. Then, and then only, the King listened.

"Go," he said, "and swiftly. Let not a breath intervene between now and your going, for life is unendurable until you return with him."

So in great haste the priest and minister set out on the way indicated by Channa, counting every instant of time they lost precious as dropped grains of pearl.

And when they were come to the forests and hills of Rajagriha, they asked their way of the wandering religious persons whom they met, and of the cave-dwelling ascetics, and to these grave persons they said:

"We are come, beseeching your aid. We serve a King like to the greatest of the Gods, and his son, beautiful as the God who pierces hearts, has forsaken us and gone out into the solitudes seeking a remedy against old age, disease, and death, a thing no man can find. Knowing this, tell us, we entreat, where we may find him."

And the ascetics replied:

"We know him and his beauty and nobleness. He is gone to the cave of Alara the Brahman that he may seek for illumination."

Scarcely giving themselves time to hear and to utter thanks those two old men, the priest and minister, hurried on.

Now as they did so the awe of the place and its quiet and the spirit of deep contemplation arising from the residence of so many holy persons fell on them, and insensibly their speed slackened, and neither said this to the other, but the same influence was upon them both, and as they had abandoned the royal chariot when the track ceased, so also they now divested themselves of the insignia of their high offices, and advanced humbly towards their destination. And as they went they saw a young ascetic seated beneath a tree, his hands folded and eyes fixed upon the running water of a stream before his feet, and he heard their steps and rising saluted them, and it was their Prince.

Surely words cannot tell how this sight moved them—they who had seen him far otherwise, who perceived about him now a difference immeasurable even in thought!

But they saluted him with more than the old obedience and being bidden took their seats beside him as the twin stars attend the moon. And about them was the vast quiet and silence and shadow of the forest.

Then choosing their words with care, as a warrior chooses the arrows that shall lose his life or save it, in turn they set before him the condition of his father the King, asking him with deep earnestness how it could be right in his eyes to abandon all his duties, inflicting sorrow worse than death upon those he loved and left.

And when they had spoken, only the little running water took up the tale, for the Prince meditated upon their words, and they dared not interpose.

After a long interval he raised his head and answered:

"This is well spoken, but I have entered the road wherein is no turning. For it is not for myself only that I seek the remedy, but for all creation. And to me the earth is filled with this thought and with this only, and however you may use the sorcery of words to bewilder me it fails. I have heard and I will again hear your plea, but this is and will be my answer— The sun, the moon, forsaking the sky, may fall to earth, the snowy mountains topple from their base, but I will never change my purpose."

And having said this he rose, and the two with him, and they, seeing that they broke themselves against rock, answered gently:

"My Prince, it is enough. No more remains to be said. We will intrude our presence on you no more, but will return to the King and lay your fixed resolution before him."

And they saluted him, and returned slowly through the forest, pausing here and there as they went to speak with the calm and untroubled inhabitants who therein sought the treasure of wisdom, eager to understand from them if possible the teaching which as the nectar of flowers draws the bee, had drawn the Prince to the homeless life. Hard was it to comprehend, and at last, sad and bewildered, they emerged from the green ocean of leaves to the light of common day and mounting the chariot, plied lash and shout hastening homeward, and thus was the last tie with Kapila broken.

And the Prince remained behind them, upborne by the love of those he had forsaken, a love too great for them and such as they to comprehend.

## CHAPTER X

THUS have I heard:

Then for patient years. Siddhartha, the Buddha to be,—struggled to the light in the forest, finding none. Surely was this the dark night of the soul wherein not so much as a star gleams in the thick and stifling midnight.

With Alara he studied long and patiently, so mastering his system of thought that the ascetics who followed Alara besought the Prince to become their master. But this he would not, for he discerned no finality in this teaching, nor any real deliverance, because desire is not extinguished even though it be for heaven, and though it be held but by a finger the ego of man is drawn again and yet again into the revolving wheel that mangles him,—the wheel of birth and death.

Therefore, abandoning the teacher Alara he went sorrowfully on to the teacher Uddaka, that wise dweller in solitude, and with him he studied in patience, hoping yet against hope that here at last might be the beginning of light.

And he mastered this system also, confronting his instructor with difficulties which could be neither explained nor overcome,—finding that Uddaka promised a glittering heaven not founded upon the Unchangeable, but transitory, vanishing, illusory. And here, too, the Way was not, nor the unchanging Law.

Then at last on his long patience dawned a certainty—that no help was in any son of man, that the riddle was too high for them and their wings fluttered lamed in the blue and awful heights where his own thoughts soared—and that even this height was not high enough. And within himself he said ;—

" What I have learned here I have learned and there is no more. The pasture is eaten bare. I will go on alone into the forests of Uruvela and there I will practise a terrible asceticism beyond all I have seen in Rajagriha, for it may be these men are right who teach that in the destruction of the body lies enfranchisement of the soul. I cannot tell, but I will pass by no opening which may set my feet in the Way."

So travelling alone (for he said in his heart: " If a traveller does not meet with one who is his better or his equal let him steadfastly keep to his solitary journey: there is no companionship with a fool") he came at last to the town of Uruvela, and when he saw the place he loved it, and long afterwards, when Enlightenment was come, he spoke of it thus:

" Then, O disciples, I thought within myself, Surely this is a place dear and delightful. The forest is wide and deep. There flows a pure river, with little creeks where a man may bathe, and fair lie the villages of the simple people. This is a good place for one in search of deliverance."

But he was very weary, and often he said to his heart:

" Long is the night to him who is awake, long is a mile to him who is tired, long is life to him who knows not the true Law. O that it would shine upon me in this gross darkness."

And there in the great woods he set himself to a cruel discipline so that other wood-dwellers marvelled at his austerities though themselves treading a painful way. And of these were in especial five, of whom more hereafter. And they established themselves within reasonable distance, hoping to learn from him when he should attain, and talking with him of great things.

So by the river in the forest composing his body and mind he set himself to contemplation, lessening his food little by little daily until he subsisted on a morsel incredible to the mind of man, and even this he would have spared had it been possible that the attenuated body could still have caged the soul. And after awhile he spoke to no man, sitting lost in far-off regions they could not enter, even controlling his breath so that scarcely could he be said to breathe at all.

So still, so motionless, he sat day-long that he became a part of nature as much as the tree that sheltered him, and the creatures of the forest moved about him unafraid. The furry mothers brought their cubs to nestle by his feet, and winged mothers lit upon his shoulders to call their broods, and at his feet the wild peacock outspread his jewelled fans, and fear was unknown in the still presence of the Bodhisattva—the Buddha-to-be.

Far and wide spread the fame of this great and noble ascetic in the woods of Uruvela, and persons would journey from the city that they might stand far off and see him lost in meditation, and when, looking timidly through the boughs, they beheld his starved body like a withered tree and his calm unseeing eyes they were moved with wonder and compassion, and went away very softly, in their hearts entreating his prayers and blessings.

But lost in deep meditation Siddhartha was beyond prayer or blessing, and whether they came or went he neither saw nor knew.

Making his way perfect through the disentangling powers of wisdom, fasting cruelly, yet not trusting in this austerity for enfranchisement, he strengthened in heart and wisdom even as his body weakened.

And first he meditated on transience, and all about him confirmed the truth, for nothing stayed but all became and passed instantly, never resting, into further becoming. About him the seasons trod their quiet round, Scarcely had the young spring burst into blossom, when, before she had leisure to mirror her beauty in the river at his feet, she was lost in the burning splendour of summer, and this passed without pause or division into the gold and orange fruitage of autumn and the passionate weeping of the rains, and so ended in the temperate sweetness of winter, there to recommence the eternal Wheel of Change.

And he thought: "There is no being, for all is becoming. On what shall we build?"

And before him the spider spun her frail thread, glittering with morning dew, lovely as a queen's garments in the pale morning gold that filtered through green leaves. And so in a moment it was gone. And he thought:

"Surely the existence of man is frailer. A blow, a breath of pestilence and he lies broken, an offence to the earth. To appear, to disappear. Such is the history of man as of the meanest of insects." And before his strained perception unrolled itself the whole vast phantasmagoria of thought like a veil hung to conceal the Permanent, the Eternal, and he could not penetrate behind it. Before him were the steps by which the creature ascends to the Source, but in the height they dissolved into vapour and dispersed into cloud and there was no way there.

And sometimes so present were the evil and pain of life to his vision, so unescapable their presence, that for a space it seemed the perfection of divine attainment was but an infinite of the first power, but evil and pain an infinite of immeasurable power, terrible in perfection. And to a lesser than the Bodhisattva this must have brought madness or despair, but strong as an eagle to the sun he outsoared the dark clouds. And unknown to himself nature spread her guards about him. In the rising of the moon was peace and her light shed tenderer dreams like the soft falling of snow, and the strong leap of the sun at dawn in the first of his three strides, was the outrush of hope—hope unfulfilled but ever on before. And the breeze was good to him, laying a cool hand on weary temples, and the singing of the river overflowed from the very heart of quiet.

And as the tapestry of life unrolled its pictures before his eyes he read its lesson. Happiness is a dream and sorrow a truth and individual life a misfortune from which impersonal contemplation is the only enfranchisement. Could this be true? Could it be possible that a barren soul, a proud and complete selfishness and heedlessness of all other sufferers than himself, disdain of the crowd and indifference to all that the vulgar covet, represent the only escape for the wise man from the entanglements of Maya—Illusion? No—a thousand times no! Better to drop into the jaws of darkness and be extinguished than remain petrified and apart in a world where men must bleed and die.

Then is goodness itself a lie? Is man the eternal dupe of words and phrases contrived to make us docile to suffering as slaves to the whip? Is hope but a watery rainbow painted on a dissolving cloud? Is the Way itself a dream begotten of Misery, the Mother, and Pride, the father—Pride that will have man think himself a something when in reality he is nothing and his fate concerns the universe as much as blown grains of sand in a whirlwind, rising and settling as aimlessly?

And at such times the Bodhisattva felt the endless turning of the Wheel within his own soul, and a vertigo of perception seized him as the Infinities gazed over his head in untroubled calm, and only the Wheel turned and turned in merciless revolution.

Then were it not better to submit to passive ignorance

and fight no more? To sink into wearied submission, accepting the lash and fetter for doom? For each life is built up of millions, and where is the redemption for its infinite littleness? Let all pass for all is nothing.

But at such times he steadied himself upon the thought of Law. Could a man nobly agree with necessity which is the other name of Law, were that no peace and enlightenment? Is not Law beheld in nature? What is this incessant changing yet unchanging series of phenomena unperplexed by self-contemplation and analysis which man sees about him. What? Is it a play—a spectacle that Brahm the Universal Spirit has set in motion for Its own delight, or is it Itself expanded throughout the Universe, and if this be so is man the one thing outside Its circumference, and if he be within it, shall he only be ignorant of the Law and agonised because he does not obey it? If man is capable of conceiving the Law surely it exists and is his and him.

So he looked down the abyss and beheld nothing but persistence in change and the infinity of infinities. Was there anywhere a fixed point? Surely only in the relation of all to Law. Therefore he hungered and thirsted for Law, forgetting the emaciation of his body and its pitiable weakness, thirsting for the Way with a deathly thirst that consumed him, rendering him incapable of all other suffering.

But though he knew full well and each day perceived more clearly that the climax of wisdom is perception of this universal Law from which nothing—no, not the very soul of man is exempt—still it evaded him. Freedom from deception he attained, diamond-clear lucidity, certainty that there is a first principle and final aim of the Universe, but the Way to touch hands with it he could not find.

Thus, having caught but a glimpse of the Absolute like a star in driven clouds, he had gained the certainty of what is not, but not as yet the knowledge of what is, and there even the majesty of the Bodhisattva's[1] intellect fell back baffled, and at last his mind became like a dimness in which thought itself lost its way and analysis stumbled, and the clear call became like the falling of a great water in which many sounds fuse into a confused roar in which nothing but mere noise is to be discerned, deafening the ears and confusing the senses.

And thus he sat for six long years, and at the end though he had discerned the perishable,the transient, the Eternal Way was far from his perception, and life rushed by him from an unknown beginning to a hopeless end, defending itself frantically for a few brief years, but in the end conquered, and the man broken in the frail edifice which is called his being.

And now he was so wasted that life hung in him by a thread worn slender as a spider's, and the fame of his terrible austerities had spread like the sound of a great bell hung in the canopy of the skies, and if he had gained what he sought all this would have counted as nothing in his eyes, but in the long six years he had not gained, and his mind tortured him because now it seemed that it broke itself and its power dispersed like a mighty wave broken on rocks and fleeing in foam and spray. And one day when he rose to his feet, still drowned in hopeless meditation, his limbs failed beneath him, and he fell and so lay exhausted, spent, believing " This is death, and I am conquered."

And it could not be otherwise for very terrible had been his austerities and later he told his disciple this.

" I remember when a crab-apple was my only daily food. I remember when a single grain of rice was my only grain of food. And my body became extremely thin and lean. Like dried withered reeds my arms and legs, my hips like a camel's hoof, like a plait of hair my

[1] The Buddha-to-be.

spine. As project the rafters of a house's roof, so raggedly stuck out my ribs. As in a deep-lying brook the watery mirror beneath appears so small as almost to disappear, so in the deep hollows of my eye-pits my eyeballs wellnigh wholly disappeared. As a gourd becomes shrivelled and hollow in the hot sun so did the skin of my head become parched. And pressing my stomach my hands touched my spine, and feeling my spine my hand felt through to the stomach. And yet with all this mortification I came no nearer to the supernatural faculty of clearness of knowledge."

So for a long time he lay in the borderland of death, and had this been the end—O Light of the World extinguished, O Sun set at dawn!—but it was not to be, and slowly, very slowly, consciousness returned, and his heavy eyelids lifted and once more he beheld the light. And he thought:

"If I could creep down to the river the waters, warm and kindly, would refresh me, and thought would perhaps return to me, and a little rest."

And painful inch by inch Siddhartha crept down to the river, supporting himself as he went by the extended hands of branches, and in a warm shallow of water, sparkling in green shade he lay, foredone, and it flowed about him gently, bringing healing.

And the five ascetics watching him from far off said to each other:

"He will die now; the ascetic Gotama will die now. It is not possible that a man so worn and exhausted should live."

And indeed, when he tried to struggle up and leave the kindly water, there was no strength in him and he could not rise. And it is told that a heavenly spirit pressed down a branch that he might reach it and support himself. This it is certain he did, laying hold on a bough which dipped over its own image in still water, and he crept up the bank, dizzily, and seated himself beneath a tree, supporting his weakness against it, with closed eyes.

And now, being refreshed, he had power to reflect, and he said within himself.

"This way of mortification has failed me also. Like other ways I have sought this beats against a shut door and there is no help in it. My body is so broken that it can no longer support the intellect. I will eat and drink and strengthen this tortured body that it may still be the servant of the higher in me, no longer complaining of its own griefs and diverting attention from the goal. For it is possible that what I have already learned has prepared the way to Right Ecstasy and that in ecstasy I may behold the beginning of the Wisdom which in all the methods I have tried has been hidden from me."

And even as he thought this the strong weakness overwhelmed him again and he could think no more.

Now, on the other side of the wood dwelt a chief herdsman, very wealthy in cattle and rice, owning land far-spreading and fertile in the rich water-meadows by the river, and he had a daughter fair and wise, named Sujata. And reaching womanhood this fair maiden had made a vow to the Tree-Spirit of the forest, saying:

"If I should wed a husband of equal rank with myself and my first-born should be a son, then would I make a noble offering every year, never forgetting the benefit." And this prayer was heard, and her first-born son lay upon her bosom.

So wishing to make her offering on the day of the full moon, she pastured a thousand cows in the woods, and with their milk she nourished five hundred cows, and with theirs two hundred and fifty, drawing life through life until at last she possessed eight cows thus fed on the strength and life of a thousand, and no purer nor stronger milk could be. And this being ready Sujata rose earlier than dawn and went to the byre with her pails, and as she came near the milk flowed in streams without milking even as when the calves crowd for their food about their mothers.

So she took it and placed it in a new vessel and added rice, and herself made a fire and cooked it. And the bubbles rose and froth, but not a drop ran over the brim, and the fire burned clear and steady without smoke or blackness. And as a man crushes golden honey from the comb that has formed about a stick—the very essence of honey—so into that pure food was infused a marvellous sustenance.

And Sujata said to her waiting-maid, Punna:

"Punna, dear girl, surely the deity is auspiciously disposed to us. The omens are good. Run therefore and get all ready beneath the tree."

And Punna answered obediently:

"Yes, lady," and ran.

And when she came to the tree, the Bodhisattva—the Buddha-to-be—sat beneath it, and it appeared to her that his body shone like light and she flushed and trembled with terror, saying:

"Good indeed are the omens, for this is the Tree-Spirit himself come to receive our offering!"

And with all her might she ran to tell this to her lady, and when Sujata heard it she cried out:

"From this day be to me as a daughter, for this great good news!"

And running to where she kept her jewels she put upon the happy Punna all those ornaments suitable to a daughter of the house. And she thought; "What more can I do? For this is a great day," and so took up a precious golden dish and into this she poured the milk-rice, and it rolled in like drops of water slipping off a lily-leaf and filled the vessel, neither more nor less.

Then covering it with a golden cover, she adorned herself with her best jewels and went stately to worship and make her offering.

So she came along the banks of the river, glad in the dawn, robed in gray like a cloud before sunrise, and about her slender wrists were bracelets of white chalcedony and the gray and white of them resembled the colours of the rounded river-bubble before it breaks, and she came as softly.

And parting the boughs she saw the Prince, his head fallen back against the tree, eyes closed and helpless hands beside him, and deep pity and veneration stirred in her heart, and seeing it was no Tree-Spirit but a holy man she thought, " May he accept it ! "

And bowing repeatedly she raised the dish in both hands, entreating his greatness, and thus offered it humbly, saying :

" Lord, accept my gift and go where it seems good to you." And he, seeing in this the accomplishment of his purpose, received it, and partook of that pure food while the happy giver watched with such delight as when a mother feeds her only child and beholds new life flow through his veins, and the very air about the Prince appeared to distil in dews of visible blessing upon her head and joy hitherto unknown possessed her noble soul. And she said :

" Lord, may your wishes prosper as mine have done ! " and so departed, caring no more for her golden dish than as if it had been an autumn leaf upon the ground.

But the five ascetics, watching far off with greedy eyes, said ;

" The ascetic Gotama has failed. He is now mere man. Like the common herd he eats and drinks. He has nothing to teach us—nothing ! Mistaken indeed were we in thinking to learn from a mere backslider ! It is done and over, and the Gods are angry with him."

So they turned their backs in scorn and departed to Benares, there to resume their austerities.

But when Sujata was gone, timidly receiving thanks, the Future Buddha arose and stood beneath the tree, refreshed in heart and body, his face shining with renewed strength, his energy swelling like a river in spate rushing rejoicing to the sea.

And he knew that that place where for six years he had pursued a vanishing truth could hold him no more, its use being ended, and he set steadfast steps toward the tree.

O Tree of Wisdom, Tree of Knowledge unsearchable, Tree whereunder the world's deliverance was attained,—through all the rain of years between our sight and thee, shall we not look back and behold and veil our faces? For beneath this Tree was Wisdom perfected.

Then taking his way, Bodhisattva begged from a man cutting grass for his cattle, an armful of pure and pliant grass, and, going onward, he saw before him that Tree of Knowledge, broad-leaved, noble, a tower of leafage, and knowing that this was where time and place meeting clasped hands, he spread the grass and seated himself with folded hands and feet beneath the pillared stems and the night came quietly down the woodland ways and veiled him from the sight of man.

# CHAPTER XI

THUS have I heard :

Yet of what follows I veil my face in writing, for it is high, holy, and beyond the mind of man to conceive, nor can it be told but in great parables, for by pictures we teach little children. It is the Arhats only,—the perfected saints,—who comprehend and can distinguish the symbol from the truth.

Bodhisattva was tempted in the wilderness. Against him that Wicked One led his hosts, strong and cunning to daunt and allure. And as our Lord sat there in peace, suddenly the calm sea, heaven-reflecting, of his mind, was tossed and torn into wild billows as in a furious storm, and foes which he had thought conquered, rose mighty against him, some most infinitely sweet, piercing the heart with a pain more to be desired than joy.

For, shaping on the dark like a picture—but real, so real that he had but to rise and enter, came the lost heaven of Kapila, where Rohini flowed in liquid light, and there in cool green shades he beheld those loveliest in whose arms once he lay. Soft bosoms, intolerably sweet after long pain and loneliness, entreated him to rest. Deep eyes, love-filled, invited. And at the last one alone drew near him and it seemed that in that one fair face was centred all beauty that was his in those far days. In one all wooed him.

" Come to me——Come to me. Dear lord, you have borne torture for long years and grief exceeding. You have hungered and thirsted and wept tears of blood and still the Way eludes you, and all was vain. There is no Way. It is delusion. Vain it must be: not thus is Paradise found. Love is heaven—there is no other." —So said the Beautiful kneeling before him, most dear and desirable, with passionate dark eyes more eloquent than music plucked on harp or sitar, words spoken between kisses and the slackening and straining of arms that are the bonds of love. On his knees he felt the warmth of her golden bosom, sun-kissed fruit for the tasting, on his hands the clasp of those little fingers that once clenched his heart.

"Put away your pale dreams of Heaven. O Prince beloved!" she pleaded. "Heaven is here and now by bright Rohini. Come, taking and giving joy. O sad and wearied, and utterly foredone, come back to us and be made whole and glad. Am I not yours? Rest in my arms. Forget the cold ascetic, and be again our Prince, our warrior. Come! Time goes swiftly and the sands of life are blown about the desert and man knows them no more."

She moved as if to draw him with her, and all her naked loveliness swam rose and gold before his eyes, long hair, brightening at the tendril-ends, caressing the slender curves of perfect feet, the smile of victory touching soft lips,—breathless beauty waiting its fruition, queen and slave of men, thinking its victory won, looking downward half amazed at its own perfection.

Then lifting her head that Beautiful regarded him in triumph as the moon rides serene over tossing waves, and lo! he sat motionless and unmoved, with eyes looking past her to a distant hope, and his face was set and calm as doom.

And suddenly, shuddering together with the sighing shudder of leaves in cold rain, the sweet shape wavered, trembled like an image in water when the rings widen outward and all is dispersed, and it was gone, for the waste night closed about it and took it.

But the garden remained—that home beloved, and a new and dearer shape wandered lonely by the river bank gazing steadfastly upward to the bright billows of the silver peaks, remote and pure as they, and she led by the hand a child. And surely he whom lust cannot conquer may unashamed kneel at the feet of love pure as the very sources of light! And his heart said "My Princess!" and almost ceased to beat, so strange, so sweet, that living bleeding memory;—and whether it was the voice of his own soul or hers he could not know,—but she seemed to shape the one word, "Beloved," and so withdrawing her gaze from the mountains, looked at him, all love, all entreaty in those sunken eyes—beauty faded by grief, but stronger a thousandfold to plead with him, and mutely she showed the child, and so stood, waiting to know his sentence whether she must live or die.

And round her like mourning shadows swept the image of his father, aged by grief and visibly stooping under the heavy burden; the gentle queen, sister of his mother who had fed him from her own bosom, wrung her hands beside him and all the faithful friends and servants who had guarded his youth; and together they were the very voice of home, and his own heart asked itself, "Have I the right to hurt these faithful ones! But what are they and myriads like them to her—my wife, my son!"

And whether he would have moved to reach her, I cannot tell, but suddenly, past all knowledge, he certainly knew that never could that great lady his wife present herself as an obstacle and a temptation, and that this was but a shift and a shape-changer not to be trusted, dangerous and cunning like the first, and steadfastly he gazed past her, his face set and calm as doom, and shrieking horribly she fled.

And then, thick as rain in *Wasa,* fell delirious dreams and delusions, and there came about him frightful things, misshapen, goblin, the very spume and smoke of the pit, and there was a noise in the air, that stupefied the brain, of shrieks and shouts and groans and terrible cries and far off wailings, and it appeared as though great spirits fought in the air about him with the black armies of the Wicked One.

And upon the night the Tempter flung a vast phantasmagoria of the power and splendour awaiting the Prince if he would but stoop to grasp them. King of the earth, throned and crowned, he saw himself. And flames shot about the pictures and huge confusions, and an ocean of terrors broke against him, and the billows threatened to overwhelm him, and he knew that did he relax but for the instant that a man blinks his eye, all were lost.

But he sat motionless, his face fixed and calm as doom, and it is told that in all the tumult not one leaf of the Tree flickered but hung still as if carved in stone. Within its shadow was calm: without tumult as when heaven and earth break together in storm.

So the strife raged about him and Lust and Love, and Power and Wealth thundered or pleaded at his ear and could not move him. And huge elemental Powers led on their armies, deep instincts from the abyss of the primeval life of man, conquering, cunning, rock-rooted, hard to be fought, beckoning, alluring, threatening. And some, robed like heavenly spirits, showed, as it were, the Way, but it was no way, and very terrible were the confusions, sights and sounds of that night of dread. Nor is it possible or lawful that all should be uttered.

But when the worst and utmost were done and endured

*and no more remained, the Wicked One and his hosts,* outwearied, ceased their torment, and very slowly the angry roar of the billows subsided and the foam of their fury stilled, and the mind of the Blessed One relaxed into peace, and the great darkness thinned as at the cold breath of dawn.

The moon and the stars reappearing shed dying light, the barriers of the dark being removed. And now—the marvel,—the marvel!

Let the Three Worlds wait in silence.

Thus have I heard.

For the east became gray, and all being now hushed, our Lord passed into deep and subtle contemplation and entered thus upon the First Stage of Ecstasy, and this was the First Watch.

And, consciousness withdrawn into the Infinite, passing through the bounds of human comprehension, seeing the world as it truly is, not as it appears, his mind moved swiftly onward and upward as the eagle soars effortless to the sun, or rather, as the swimmer daring the current is caught up and carried strongly and without volition to his desired end. For, be it known, this world about us is far other than it appears, and with enlightenment we pass free from the fetters of illusion, and in this enlightenment we behold the world about us no longer as it appears but as it truly is.

And in this Perception he beheld his past lives and all his former births, with their gains and losses, their sins and purities, as they passed steadily onward and led him inevitably to the Tree; seeing all at once as a picture.

And soaring higher, carried ever more swiftly onward, ever more profoundly withdrawn, in the second watch, *he beheld with diamond-clear perception all that lives,* and the round of birth and death of all mankind, hollow all and false and transient, built upon nothingness—

*the piers and fabric of a dream; and saw before* him erring creatures born and born again to die, the righteous and the evil heirs alike of pain self-inflicted, and stabbed with daggers their own hands have forged.

And he saw the transient heavens gained through desire, won through righteousness that craves reward, and beheld these longer-lived than the joys of earth yet transient also, for he who desires the joys of an individual heaven and pays down righteousness as the coin of its price, he too is still held within the pitiless fetters of craving, though it be for heaven, and nothing rooted in desire is eternal, but must pass and be done.

And he saw the hells that, gorged with suffering, yet again yield up their prey to the weary round of rebirth, and lo—heaven and hell and earth empty and vain, the Wheel of Birth and Death revolving evermore, hopeless and without delay or stay, now heaven-high, now low as earth, but ever and ever a whirling Wheel without rest. And in the third watch there came Perception higher still and our Lord entered upon the deep apprehension of Truth.

And in this the secrets of birth and death were apparent and he became assured that age and death have their source in birth and are rooted in it as trees in the ground, for the body and earthly self implicate man in all evils, divided thus from the Source, and, in a word, life in this world of ignorance, is suffering. For here men walk blinded with ignorance, not knowing whence nor whither, and the high things move veiled about them and are not seen.

And as to rebirth, he saw that its cause is in deeds done and thoughts thought in former lives.

Swept on and up in ecstasy, perception becoming ever clearer, he beheld the so-called soul-self of man unravelled into its component parts and laid before him like the unwoven threads of a garment, and behold in these was no durability nor immortality, for there is but one Immortal, one Infinite, and the man who claims his own, his separate immortality, is dying and reborn through the ages and but the fierce desire of life gives him its simulacrum and the long-linked chain of births and deaths and griefs immeasurable.

So then, swept on and up in ecstasy, he beheld the causes of the long-linked chain of existence stretching from Infinite to Infinite.

And these are they, and this is the lineage of suffering :

Contact brings forth sensation.
Sensation brings desire.
Desire produces the clinging to shows and illusions.
Clinging to shows and illusions produces deeds.
Deeds engender birth.
Birth produces age and death.

And this is the weary round, the offspring of Ignorance repeated in the endless turning of the Wheel, the dragging of a lengthening chain of births. For the ignorant man, desiring the things that are worthless, transient, illusory, seeing about him false shows instead of the high things which are real, creates in himself a passion which in turn creates more and more dangerous illusions, and thus is his own victim. But when false desire dies, illusions end, and Ignorance, dispersing like the night, gives place to the Sun of Enlightenment and the world lies about such a man as it truly is. And he *knows*, being no more the prisoner of time and space and their brood of follies, for Ignorance, the true cause of all ill, in him is dead, and he has reached the Universal and is All and One.

And having thus perceived the world as it is, our Lord

was perfected in wisdom, and shows and illusions being ended for him, there died in him that false self which will have all for its own; never again to be born, utterly at an end,—even that false ego shut in the prison of itself. And in him was completed the destruction of craving and evil desire, as a fire goes out for lack of fuel. For the man in whom is no separation from the Source, or in whom is no ignorance, how shall he desire that which has no eternity but is transient as a morning dream? And over him Desire and Death—which indeed are one—had no more dominion.

Thus first he found the way of perfect knowledge, and in the broad east the onrushing of the sun's golden wheels was heard afar.

So he reached at last the unfathomable source of Truth, beholding past, present, and future as one, having passed beyond the glimmer of the six senses into true perception, no longer gazing through a narrow window, but about and around him the wide horizon—and the Unutterable.

Illumined with all wisdom sat the Buddha, the Perfected One, having at last attained, and the light strengthened and grew in rapture. And about him the world lay calm and bright and a soft breeze lifted the leaves.

And for seven days and nights sat our Lord beneath the Tree, lost in contemplation of the World as it Is, submerged in the ocean of love, having entered the Nirvana, most utterly at peace; and day and night—or what men call such—made their solemn procession about him unheeded, for he was lost in bliss, and his heart said:

"Now, resting here, have I attained my birth-weary heart's desire, having traversed many lives to this goal. Now have I slain the self, and the fetters are broken, and not for myself alone."

And lifting up his voice he cried aloud this song of triumph in the hearing of all worlds.

"Many a house of life
Has held me, seeking ever that which wrought
These prisons of the senses, sorrow-fraught,
Sore was my ceaseless strife.
But now,
Thou Builder of the body-prison,—Thou!
I know thee! Never shalt thou build again
These walls of pain,
Nor raise the roof-tree of deceits, nor lay
Fresh rafters on the clay.
Broken the House is, and the ridge-pole split,
Delusion fashioned it.
Safe pass I hence, deliverance to attain."[1]

For now he knew that the builder of the prison, the cause of rebirth, the hinderer from the Peace was his own false self, the dreamer of dreams, the creator of false desires and illusions, and in him this false self was dead, and only the true, the Self that is mysterious and high and One with the One survived.

And next, sending his sight through the invisible (for when enlightenment is attained all bars of time and space fall and man is no longer blinded by his eyes and deafened by his ears), he considered all that live, and like a swelling tide there rose in him compassion for their darkness and misery, and in deep contemplation he considered how to gain deliverance for them also, and with this came the thought:

"Shall I teach? And how? For the Truth is beyond all speech, and who shall understand?" And he said:

[1] For this verse I have used Edwin Arnold's translation slightly modified.

"How can they believe the world is other than it seems and the very sea and sky and mountains far differing from what they have supposed? And they the prisoners of Ignorance?" And a deep voice from the Divine within and without him answered:

"O let your heart most loving be moved into pity toward the people, most ignorant, toiling amid deathly illusions to a goal unknown."

And as this purpose rooted and flowered within him—a mighty blossom opening its chalice of perfume to all worlds and heavens, the dawn of the seventh day broke resplendent, as it were a new heaven and a new earth, and it was light.

Light also within him and a great flooding of light, for not only was the Way opened but the steps now lay clear before him—the Noble Eightfold Path whereby men setting one foot before the other achieve the first heights, the true Self developing as does the body from lowly beginnings to great ends and royalties, but all in order and gradually, each step rising by the stepping stones of dead selves in dead lives to higher.

O peace: O bliss inexplicable, not to be confounded with others, but singular, lovely, and alone! Not in the heavens, unattainable save by the strength of Gods, but within reach of all who set their faces to the heights in true and steadfast endeavour, proceeding step by step in love and patience. For the lowly, the little children of the Law, as for the wise and noble. For he who is ruler over a few things in this life shall in lives to come be ruler over many, so he be found faithful. And at the last—not the dewdrop lost in the ocean, but the ocean drawn into the dewdrop and eternal Unity.

And in his heart this thought arose.

"I will proclaim accordingly the way unto the further shore!"

As he saw it, so he told it: He the stainless, the Very Wise, the Passionless, the Desireless Lord; for what reason should he speak falsely?

Thus, flooded with sunshine and bathed in peace sat the Perfect One.

## CHAPTER XII

Now as the Blessed One sat beneath the Tree in the Dawn, two merchants bound on their way passed through the wood, and within them spoke the Voice of Wisdom, saying:

"In this wood, outspread upon the spurs of the mountain, dwells a Rishi—a wise ascetic—deeply to be reverenced; go then and make him an offering."

And with joy they went, glad in the opportunity of righteousness, and found him enthroned beneath the Tree, laving his feet in the ripples of the Sea of Bliss; and wth reverence they placed food in his bowl, a simple gift and good; and they were respectfully silent while he ate, but when they saw that the Exalted One, his need over, had washed his bowl and hands in the mountain stream, they bowed their heads to his feet, saying:

"We who are here take refuge in the Perfect One and his Law. May the Blessed One accept us as his adherents from this day forth throughout our life, who have taken refuge in him."

And they were accepted as lay followers and went on their business rejoicing in peace; and these were the first persons who accepted the Law, with faith in the One Enlightened and his teaching, for as yet the communion of the Order was not. And their names were Bhallika and Tapussa.

Yet, having risen, he paused, and again seated himself in meditation, for he doubted again whether it were either wise or possible to make known the great Law to the world.

And into the mind of the Exalted One yet retired in solitude, came this thought.

"I have penetrated this deep truth of the abandonment of the imprisoning self, hard to be perceived, difficult to grasp. Man moves in an earthly sphere, and there has he his place and delights, tapestried about with illusions real indeed to the dim feelers of his poor senses. For such it will be hard to grasp this matter, the chain of causes and effects, for man sees the effect but not the cause. And very hard to grasp are withdrawal from earthly illusions, extinction of desire, cessation of longing, and the deep mysterious Peace. Should I now preach the Law, it would gain nothing—grief and weariness would be the only fruit of labour. The truth remains hidden from men absorbed by hate and greed. It is deep and difficult, veiled from the coarse mind. How shall he apprehend it whose thought moves in the darkness of earthly preoccupations? Or see, who dwells in the World of Forms?"

And this was without doubt the last, the uttermost temptation of that Wicked One, and the subtlety of it stirred a vibration in the highest of the Divine Beings, and this thought arose.

"Truly the world is lost, truly the world is undone if the heart of the Perfect One be set on abiding in peace without revealing the Law."

And instantly this Divine thought was light in the heart of the Exalted One and its symbol was that he beheld a Divine Being who raised his folded hands before him, saying:

"May it please the Perfect One to preach the Law! There are a few whose eyes are not dimmed with the dust of earth. They will see. They will hear. Open, O Wise One, the door of Eternity. He who stands on the mountain peaks looks out over all peoples. Go forth to Victory."

Then, hearing this voice in his ears, the Exalted One turned the gaze of perfect enlightenment upon the world, and he beheld this:

As on a lotus stem bearing the lotus blossoms of ivory, some flowers do not rise out of the water but are below the surface, and others float on the calm surface, and others rise high, reflecting themselves in its mirror, so are men—some pure. and some impure, some noble and some ignoble, some strong in mind and intellect, others weak and dull,—but all needing what they are qualified to take of the light of wisdom. And perceiving this, he replied as it were to the Divine Voice:

"It was because I believed the toil fruitless, Holy One, that I have not yet uttered the Word."

And the Divine Voice perceived what would be, saying:

"It is done. The Perfect One will preach the Law," and the matter being thus ended the Divine Voice returned to its source and the Buddha passed onward in majesty, musing on the first means whereby the Law should be made known. And since a man owes deep duty to his teachers who, if they have not opened the gate have yet directed him in the Path, his thought hovered first over Alara and Uddaka the Brahmans,—but the diamond-clear inward sight revealed to him that in the six years of his asceticism they were dead.

And next he remembered the five ascetics who had scorned him when in starving he had tasted of the food offered by the lady Sujata, thinking "These shall be the first fish I catch in my net!"—and because they had betaken themselves to Benares, he resolved that leaving the Forest of Enlightenment he would go to that great and ancient city bathing her feet in holy Ganges and there for the first time make known the Pearl he had found.

So, alone in the wood, he arose from beneath the Tree and turning regarded it steadfastly, saying:

"O Tree, because of this, many generations of men as yet unmanifested on earth, shall hold your name in honour and a leaf of you shall be precious. Rejoice therefore and accept the sunshine and rain gladly, knowing that life is in the least of your leaves for ever and ever."

Then with eyes deep and kind, shedding light, as it were, about him, steadfast in noble composure did he advance through the Wood of Wisdom, taking the way to Benares, strengthened as one fed on food divine. And beside the way to Benares, journeying on in peace, he met a young and haughty Brahman, proud in the possession of his greatness, whose name was Upaka, and as this man went he repeated the mystic word "Aum," of which the three letters are the Threefold and the word the One, and in this he put his faith. And seeing the Exalted One passing by, rapt in meditation, he cried aloud with scorn:

"Ha, Master,—what constitutes the true Brahman?" hoping to trip him in his answer. And from the heart of his calm the Exalted One replied:

"To put away all evil, to be pure in thought, word and deed, to transcend pride and desire,—this it is to be a true Brahman."

And the answer astonished the proud young man, and turning suddenly he looked into the face of the Perfect One and said slowly:

"How comes it that your face is so beautiful, shining like the full moon reflected in water, your form so stately? And whence the peace that surrounds you? What is your noble tribe, and who your master? Here, in this country, where each man struggles to find the Way, what is your way ?"

And, glad at heart, the Perfect One answered :

"Happy the solitude of him who is full of joy, who has seen the truth. Happy he who in all the wide world has no ill-will, self-restrained and guided. Happy—happiest is freedom from the pride of the thought *I am I*. No honourable tribe have I,—no Teacher. I go alone and content."

And the Brahman heard in great astonishment, for much as he had heard of religion it was not this. And he said, hesitating :

"And where, sir, are you bound ?" And the World-Honoured replied :

"I desire to set revolving the Wheel of the Excellent Law, and therefore I go to the great and ancient city of Benares, to give light to them that sit in darkness and to open the gate of true Immortality to men."

And when the Brahman Upaka heard this his pride was revolted and he was angry that a man should assume to himself such mastership, and he replied curtly :

"Reverend person, your way lies onward," and struck into the opposite path, yet as he went, he stopped, proceeded, stopped again, lost in thought, for there was that in the occurrence which startled him from his equanimity. So the moment goes by us, and we do not know it ! But the Blessed One, proceeding quietly day by day, came at last to Benares, to the Deer Park of Isipatana where now dwelt the five ascetics who had scorned him. And there they sat practising the weary round of their austerities, not knowing that the Perfect One who approached them had discovered the way that leads from the world of sorrowful becoming and the flowing stream of transiency into the world of happy being where all is beheld as it is.

For to the man who knows not the way all things flow and pass in unreality and nothing abides; but the foot of him who has thus attained is set on the Eternal and in That is no motion nor any change.

So when they saw him coming the five ascetics were angry, and they said to one another:

"Friends, here comes the ascetic Gotama [using in contempt his family name] he who eats rich food, who lives in self-indulgence and has given up his quest. Let us show him no respect nor rise up to meet him, nor take his alms-bowl nor cloak from him. Let us only give him a seat as we would to any person, and he can sit down if he likes."

But the nearer the Exalted One came to the five the more did the majesty of his presence precede him, and the less could they abide by their resolution. Slowly they rose, and went forward, and one took the cloak and alms-bowl—another brought a seat, a third brought water, and accepting the water the Blessed One sat down and bathed his weary feet.

And then they addressed him as "Friend" and "Gotama," but he replied:

"It is not seemly, monks, that you should address Him who has thus Attained as 'Friend' and 'Gotama.' For I am now the Enlightened. Open your ears: I teach you the Law. If you will learn, the Truth shall meet you face to face."

But, still in much doubt, they said:

"If you were not able, friend Gotama, to attain full knowledge by mortification of the body, is it likely you can attain it by self-indulgence and a worldly life?"

And thus replied the Blessed One:

"Monks, I do not live in self-indulgence although I torture my body no more. Nor have I forsaken my quest. Open your ears. Found is deliverance from death and illusion!"

And because the five still doubted, the Blessed One said to them:

" Tell me, monks,—when we dwelt in the forest, did I ever before speak to you in this manner ? "

And they said:

" Sir, never."

And he drew them with power irresistible, and opening their ears they heard like men amazed.

So, with the five about him, the Perfect One spoke the first words of the Teaching of the Law, the first ever heard in this world,—and where the last shall be spoken who can tell ? But it is needful that all to whom their happy Karma allows it should hear and ponder these words for in them is all truth. Now this is the high teaching in the Deer Park of Isipatana, as dusk came on and the shadows.

And it is told in the ancient scriptures that the very evening appeared to bow at the knees of the Exalted One—the World-Honoured, that she might hear his word. Like a maiden she came, the stars the pearls about her throat, the gathering dark her braided hair, the deepening vastness of space her cloudy robe. For a crown had she the holy heavens where dwell divine spirits. The Three Worlds were her body, her eyes were as blue lotus blossoms opening to the moonlight and her voice of stillness as the distant murmur of bees. To worship and to hear the Perfect One this lovely maiden came.

And though our Lord spoke in the Pali tongue each man heard his own. And thus said the Blessed One, the Tathagata, He who has thus Attained:

" Monks, there are two extremes which he who would follow my attainment must shun. The one is a life of pleasure devoted to desire and enjoyments. That is base, ignoble, unworthy, unreal, and is the Path of Destruction. The other is the life of self-mortification and torture. It is gloomy, unworthy, unreal. It is nothing and leads to nothing. But hear and be attentive, monks, for I have found the Middle Way which lies between these two, the way which in a spiral of eight stages ascends the Mount of Vision even to the summit where dwells the glory of the Peace.

This is the Noble Eightfold Path, and the stages in their order. Right Comprehension. Doubts and wrong views and mere opinions must be laid aside. The man must perceive the distinction between the Permanent and the Transient. He must behold facts behind hypotheses. Realisation of the need of truth is the attitude for its reception. This is the first stage.

Right Resolution. This is the will to attain, based on self-discipline and the vision which has perceived that attainment of perfect knowledge is possible. This is the second stage.

Right Speech. This is the first step in the practice of self-discipline. Indiscretion, slander, abuse, and bitter words are forbidden. Only such words must be uttered as are kind, pure, true. This is the third stage.

Right Conduct. Deeds which are blameless, true, and noble. These only must be done. Put away all thought of gain or reward here or hereafter, for the motive is the deed. Retaliation is dead. Impulse cannot exist with discipline. Deeds actuated by likes and dislikes are forbidden,—let each action be guided by inward Law irrespective of whom it concerns. Act only from this Law which is in its highest Love and Pity, and very swiftly will come the insight to distinguish which deeds are in harmony with the Law and which gainsay it,—and that blessedness will follow which the doer has not thirsted to gain or garner. This is the fourth stage.

Very difficult to climb are the two stages of Right

Speech and Right Conduct, but, when they are surmounted, fair and wide and noble is the prospect seen from those heights, and very great self-mastery is gained.

Right Living. And this includes the right means of earning a livelihood, for there are means a man cannot follow and maintain his integrity and purity. Let him take heed to avoid these dangerous circumstances, and which they may be that man's mind shall declare to him if he have trodden the Four First Stages. Such a man cannot be in doubt. And so is the learner become a Master. This is the Fifth stage.

Right Effort. Now, loving, wise, and enlightened, he apportions all his strength to wise purpose, fully comprehending his deed and its aim. He who has reached this noble stage does all, whether eating or drinking, sleeping or waking, working or resting, in harmony with the great Law, for in his obedience he is perfect; and the Law is his life, nor does he need to consider longer than while a man in health need count his heart-beat. And this is the Sixth Stage.

Right Meditation. This is the right state of a mind at peace. He considers only the truth, and having utterly abandoned the thought of self he is clear in perception, having slain illusion and stood face to face with Reality as a man speaks with a friend. He is the Knower of Truth. More, he *is* the Truth, and this is the Seventh Stage.

Right Rapture. This the state of a mind at peace. At peace indeed, for what is left for grief? Nothing is here to wail, nothing but what must quiet us. Doubt and fear, trouble and confusions are dead. Groundless beliefs, false hopes and fears are forgotten, and in this stage is the attainment of the Peace which passes understanding. This is the Eighth Stage, from which, having attained, a man cannot fall.

But, monks, you may ask, what is the cause from which springs the need for the Noble Eightfold Path? It is this. Hear the Four Noble Truths.

Birth is the cause of suffering, for life is suffering, passing through all the stages of grief from birth to death. This is the first Truth. The cause of birth is the thirst for living, leading from birth to birth, fed by the lust of the flesh, the lust of the eye, the pride of life. This is the second Truth.

The cure of the cause of birth is the extinction of this thirst for living by complete extinction of wrong desire, letting it go, expelling it; giving it no room. This is the third Truth.

And the fourth Truth is the Noble Eightfold Path. These are the four Truths.

So by the truth of suffering, monks, my eyes were opened to these conceptions and judgment and vision were opened in me. Not by sacrifice nor mortification nor prayer, but by that which a man has in himself is the Way of Deliverance opened. And as long as I did not know this I had not received enlightenment. But now have I attained, and deliverance is secured, and henceforth I shall no more go out into birth and death. Death has no more dominion over me."

This is the first Teaching and it was spoken in the Deer Park at Isipatana,—and the five ascetics sat about to hear, and borne on these great words their eyes were opened and with joy they accepted the Law, and the chief of them, Kondanna, since called "Kondanna the Knower," entreated the Lord that he would receive them as disciples, and in these words he received them:

"Draw near, monks, well preached is the Doctrine. Walk in purity to the goal of the end of all suffering."

And further he taught them of the transiency and

impermanence of all earthly things and of the Truth that lies beyond when the world is apprehended as it is, free of illusion, free of the fleeting apprehensions of the senses, and knowing this, they entered into the Peace.

And when it was ended the darkness was deep about them and the night of rest was come, for they had passed from the world of forms into the universe of perception and realisation.

# PART III

# CHAPTER XIII

So for a time the World-Honoured dwelt in the Deer Park of Isipatana, and men came eagerly to hear him, for his teachings resembled none they had heard as yet and delivered them from the yoke of priests in teachings and beliefs which if they could not inwardly accept made them verv sorely afraid of the anger of the Gods and compelled much ceremonial and expiation.

But He, who has thus Attained, the Tathagata, taught them thus:

"No priest, no God, can deliver a man. By himself is evil done, by himself he endures the shame and pain. By himself and his own will and struggle he becomes pure. There is none can save a man but himself—No, none in heaven or earth. It is he himself who must walk the Way: The Enlightened can but show it. Therefore where and how can a priest aid you?"

And this appeared to them a most wonderful doctrine, inspiring with great courage and resolution, and looking upon each other they said:

"If it be thus, and a man holds deliverance in the hollow of his hand, it can be done. To-day, brother, let us take the first step."

And so the Exalted One taught them to break the fetter of the delusion of self—the delusive belief that the individual self is real and self-existent. For to abide contented in the prison of this apparent self not looking forward to its expansion into the Universal self is the shadow of egoism and egoism is the mother of sin.

And he broke off them the fetter of the belief that outward righteousness of conduct will deliver a man, or that safety lies in rites and ceremonies, for truly a man can never say within himself, " I have placated the Gods and may now go my way in peace."

Now at this time there was in the great city of Benares a noble youth named Yasas, son of a rich man, master of one of the city guilds, and on this son his parents had lavished every good thing. He possessed a house of cool shades for summer, and another for the season of the rains. And his houses were full of delicately beautiful dancing girls, jewelled and perfumed, and what pleasure was absent, whether of food or wines, or music or any other?—None indeed, for the rich merchants dwell in luxury resembling that of kings.

And at first all this was good to him and he asked no more; but fulfilled every desire on the instant. There are men so embruted that this will content them until bodily power fails, but the noble youth Yasas was not of these.

And suddenly in the midst of his pleasures deep loathing fell upon him and secret disgust because he had sounded the utmost of pleasure and no more or better remained, and it was like vomit in his mouth, revolting to his soul.

And one night as he lay among his women, and they, abandoned to sleep, surrounded him, lovely as maidens of Mount Sumeru, he leaned against his silken cushions and the hall became hateful to him and he could no more endure it, but rose softly and put on his gilded shoes and went out into the midnight gardens where dripping dew impearled every leaf and blossom and glittered in pure moonlight, and the cool and calm were excellent. And he walked under the black and white light and dark of a long path by trees whose carven leaves hung like sculptured stone in the stillness of the air and their shadows flitted like dreams over his robes and face as he went, meditating upon the unspeakable weariness and distaste that filled him and the uncomforted wretchedness of youth that in all the world can find no good. And he said aloud:

"O my heart, how oppressive it is! O, my soul, the speechless weariness! Who in all the world shall show me any good."

So, in his walking, he came to the gate of the garden and it stood wide open and the porter lay drowned in sleep, his face hidden from the moonlight, and there was none to see who came or went, and Yasas wandered on through dewy ways and silver pools of moonlight, not knowing where he went, having fled the house because he could no longer endure his despair. And as he came at last to the Deer Park of Isipatana the darkness began to thin for dawn.

And so it was that the Lord had risen from sleep and walked beneath the trees of Isipatana in meditation and he saw a young man coming, and in the great stillness heard him say:

"O my grief, how deep is my wretchedness," and he pitied him, for he himself had been a rich young man, and he knew his heart.

So, taking his seat, the Blessed One said aloud:

"Sir, you are weary, but I hold in my hand a life that is neither grievous nor wretched. Sit down beside me and hear the Law. This doctrine, Yasas, is not oppressive. This is not afflicting."

And Yasas, seeing beneath the trees a young man of royal bearing and beauty like to but surpassing his own, yet robed as a monk, was startled. Nor could he refuse, and he took off his gilded shoes and having saluted the stranger with courtesy sat down beside him, and in the quiet of the coming dawn, the Blessed One spoke. And first he spoke of the misery, worthlessness and ruin of lust, of the strong calm of renunciation, of the high way of the Law, and as he heard, in place of burning disgust there flowed into the heart of Yasas the refreshing streams of wisdom, as when a man sets hot and travel-worn feet in the coolness of a pellucid lake. And there was that fruit of former births within the noble youth which drew him to high things, even as a pure silken fabric is with ease dyed a noble colour.

And the Lord saw this, and knowing his heart elate and ready he then set before him the Four Noble Truths of Sorrow and the Noble Eightfold Path, and the eyes of Yasas were opened and conquering joy possessed him, and the sun rose within and without him in splendour, and it was day.

Then Yasas arose and said:

"It is impossible that I should return to my former life for I see it now unreal and foolish, a tale told by a madman signifying nothing. Let me receive from the Lord ordination and admission to the Order that I may spend eternity in acquiring knowledge."

And the Blessed One answered.

"Come, monk. The Doctrine is well taught. Lead henceforward a new life."

So he was received into the Order; and the false ego died in him.

And presently his father, the rich guild-master, came running, eagerly asking whether the Exalted One had seen his son pass that way. And thus he fell into talk with the Tathagata (even with Him who has thus Attained), and he too became ensnared by that great Presence and great Doctrine as a bee with perfumed mogra blossoms, for sweet, sweet is the Truth to them who are akin to it; and last he exclaimed:

"Wonderful, great sir, most wonderful! This truly

is showing the way to the lost and setting a lamp in darkness. I take refuge in the Lord, the Law, and the Assembly. May the Lord take me as a lay disciple henceforth, while my life lasts."

And he was accepted, and looked upon his son, now divested of jewels and clad in the yellow robe with bared shoulder, and the Exalted One said to him:

"Is it possible, householder, that Yasas, the noble youth, should return to a worldly life of lusts and pleasure?"

And he replied:

"Sir, it is not possible. It is gain to Yasas the noble youth, that his mind should be set free. Will the Exalted One consent this day to take food with me, with Yasas beside him as a younger brother?"

And the Buddha by silence gave his consent. So were those two freed from the bonds of desire and entered into the Peace. For they knew the Truth, and this was their desire.

> "From the unreal lead me to the real,
> From darkness to light.
> From death to immortality."

And of the light companions of Yasas, many allured to the teaching by his joy, heard and were glad and followed, and many more, too many to tell, women as well as men (for the Blessed One welcomed women also, regarding neither sex nor caste) sought the Deer Park of Isipatana and followed the Law.

And these are the commandments they accepted, and be it understood that the first five only are binding upon laymen and women, but the whole ten are binding on the Brotherhood, and they may not marry nor take upon them the householder's life while they are a part of the Order.

1. Thou shalt not destroy life.
2. Thou shalt not take what is not given.
3. Thou shall abstain from unchastity.
4. Thou shalt not lie nor deceive.
5. Thou shalt abstain from intoxicating drinks.
6. Thou shalt eat temperately and not after noon.
7. Thou shalt not behold dancing, singing, music, or plays.
8. Thou shalt not wear garlands, perfumes, ornaments and adornments.
9. Thou shalt not use high nor luxurious beds.
10. Thou shalt not accept gold and silver.

And now, when sixty of the disciples had attained complete enlightenment, it came into the mind of the Blessed One that the time was come to send them forth into the world to spread the high Doctrine, and he said to them:

"See now!—You have passed the river and reached the shore of peace, and for you birth and death are no more, being one with the Unchanging. Go then through every country, teach those who have not heard. Make known the Teaching, lovely in its origin, its progress, and most lovely in its consummation. Make it known both in the spirit and the letter, Go!—each one travelling by himself (But later they went two together) rescue and receive. I too will go—for the work is begun."

But Yasas he would not send out into the world, for his aged parents had need of him in Benares.

Then the sixty having in all reverence received his commands went forth, for in those days books were not and each man was a book of the Law, and the Lord himself went on to Gayasisa, followed by many who had been ascetics. And great joy went with them and a shining peace, for like a swelling wave exaltation lifted their souls so that each looking on the other was glad.

It was at Gayasisa that the Exalted One uttered the great Fire teaching.

And the cause of it was this. As he and his disciples sat on the Elephant Rock near Gaya, with the wide and pleasant valley of Rajagriha outspread beneath them, a jungle fire broke out across the valley and they watched it, and thus spoke the World-Honoured; drawing a lesson as they looked.

"Everything about and within us, brethren, is on fire, and how? The senses are afire with passion, hate and illusion. The mind with its perception and sensations is afire with passion, hate and illusion, betrayed and deceived every way. Every approach by which a man beholds and comes in contact with life is afire with passion and illusion, and these all in turn supply fuel to the burning. And the wise and noble disciple, perceiving this, is indifferent to the lies of the senses and the sensations arising from them whether pleasant or unpleasant. He is indifferent to mental perceptions whether pleasant or unpleasant. And this indifference extinguishes the fire and cools its ashes and deprives it of fuel and thus frees him from passion and illusion, and being free he recognises his freedom. He clings no more to the individual and selfish self. Rebirth is destroyed, the life of pure duty and love is lived, and the world has no more wherewith to tempt him."

And many heard and accepted the teaching and found peace, having seen that behind this false world of illusion created by the senses lies the true world of things as they are.

And from Gaya, the World-Honoured, followed by his disciples, went onward to the city of Rajagriha, the chief town of King Bimbisara, and with him went Kassapa, a great disciple, and wise, who had been a worshipper of the pure element of the sacrificial fire until he had heard the teaching of the Buddha, and so great and wise was this man that many of the people of Rajagriha doubted which was the Master and which the disciple. But the Exalted One, willing to honour the disciple, addressed him thus in presence of the King and people.

"Welcome, great Master, welcome! Rightly have you distinguished Law, winning the highest wisdom. And now, as a wealthy noble displays his treasures to bring forgetfulness of sorrow to those who love beauty, so do you!"

And it is told that immediately Kassapa, composing himself into ecstasy, was raised up in the air before the eyes of all and this wonderful sight drew their eyes in adoration of so mighty a marvel, so that with different mouths but in language one they magnified the Buddha, exclaiming:

"Let the World-Honoured be our teacher. We are his disciples."

And perceiving them eager to hear, he addressed them on the false self, the lying, that is nothing but claims all within and without as fuel for its greed.

Hear and be wise.

"The mind, the thought and all the senses are subject to the law of life and death, and, understanding the self and the transient things of which it is compounded and how the thought and senses act, there is no room left for this individual *I* nor any ground for this *I*, for it is this belief in *I* which gives rise to all sorrows binding us as with cords to the world of illusion. But when a wise man knows there is no such *I* and that it does not exist, the bonds are severed.

Of those who believe in this false *I*, some say it endures beyond death, some say it perishes. Grievous is the error of both. For if they say this *I* is perishable, then all the fruit of their striving perishes and there is no hereafter, and who can call this deliverance?

And if they say this greedy *I* is immortal, then in

the midst of all life and death in this world of illusion there is but one identity that is not born and does not die—even this greedy *I*. And if the one immortal thing is this greedy *I* which arrogates all to itself then is it the one thing in the whole Universe that is self-perfect, and there is no need of high and noble deeds,—this greedy self is lord and master of all, and what need to strive for what is already done? For if this greedy *I* is lasting and imperishable then can it never be changed.

But when a man has learned there is *no* greedy *I*, that it does not exist, that it can do nothing, is but an illusion, then, freed, he passes on to the wider outlook, the nobler knowledge, and he passes on also in other lives the same yet not the same, as the shoot springs from the seed, and the seed is not the shoot, and yet is not different. Such is the birth of all that lives. Learn therefore that this *I* does not exist, and the illusion of it conceals That which Is."

So the World-Honoured, the Happy One, great and glad, addressed the King and people, and very joyfully they heard, understanding that in the egoism of the *I* lives all curse, all ignorance.

And the King became a lay follower and throughout his life was faithful, and many of the noble young men about him believed also, and many of the people.

It was here too, in happy Rajagriha, that the Perfect One gained the two greatest of his Arhats, his perfected saints, and thus it befell.

On a day to be remembered, it so chanced that Assaji, a disciple, walked in the streets, collecting alms of food in his bowl, and he walked in the shade, in the yellow robe, one shoulder bare, composed and with majesty, musing as he went. And he was thus observed by a young Brahman of noble birth who was studying spiritual things in the city under a teacher, and when he saw him the dignity of his serene presence moved the heart of the Brahman Sariputta, and he thought:

"Surely this is one who has already attained the way of purity! I will go and ask him in whose name he has renounced the world and by what Law. Not yet, for he is collecting alms, but presently."

Therefore he watched, and when the venerable Assaji had received food from the householders he turned back, and Sariputta approached him with a courteous salutation, which having concluded, he said:

"Friend, your eyes are shining, your colour pure and clear. Great is your composure. In whose name have you renounced the world and who is your honourable Master?"

"Friend, my master is the Son of the Sakya House, the descendant of Kings; I am but a novice. As yet I cannot tell the great heights of the Law, but in a few words I can give its spirit."

"Be it so, friend. Instruct me."

And musing a moment, Assaji said this:

"The Perfected One teaches how existences apparently separate are dependent upon One Cause, how they depend upon one another, their apparent separateness springing from ignorance and illusion as its cause, and how these existences can be ended and the Truth of Unity appear. This is the teaching of the Son of the Sakyas."

And as he heard these words, suddenly their implications and how they affect all within and without us and the whole Universe, flashed into the clear vision of Sariputta, and he understood as a consequence:

"Whatever is subject to the law of beginning that also is subject to the law of decay, and how should the *I* be excepted? There is but one Unchanging, motionless and eternal, of which I am part."

And deeply moved, he said to Assaji:

"If the teaching were nothing else but this you have at any rate overpassed suffering. That which many ages have not seen is revealed to us now."

And leaving Assaji, who pursued his way in peace, Sariputta hastened with winged feet to his friend and fellow-student Moggalana, and Moggalana seeing him cried out:

"Your eyes are shining. Your colour is pure and clear. Have you then found deliverance from death?"

"I have found it. I have found it."

And standing there breathless he told him of Assaji and his words, and on the great mind of Moggalana, strong in clear perception, flashed also the truth of the nonentity of the greedy *I*, and unable to delay, panting for the truth, they left the ascetic who taught them, and hurried to the wood where the Perfect One taught sitting among his disciples, and when he saw the two young Brahmans approach full of eagerness and awe, he said to those about him. "Welcome these two, for they shall be my greatest—the one unsurpassed for wisdom, the other for supernormal power."

And he himself welcomed them with joy, seeing that they would stand about him as bright stars about the moon.

So when they had told him their case and heard his words, he said:

"Come, monks, the Doctrine is well taught! Lead henceforward the pure life for the extinction of suffering," and thus received them to be his own.

And shortly after this he founded the Sangha, the Brotherhood, formally, and drew up the first code for its governance.

And the number of his followers grew and increased mightily, for not only the people but many of the noble youths of the Kingdom of Maghada joined themselves to this most noble young man, the Son of the Sakyas, so much so that some of the people were angry and said

"The ascetic Gotama is come to bring childlessness and widowhood and the decay of families," and they made a verse that was repeated in the streets,—

> "The great monk has come through the wood-ways:
> he sits on the hill,
> And whom will he steal from us next,
> for he takes whom he will?"

And his disciples hearing this verse went to the Exalted One and repeated it, dwelling on the anger of some of the people. But the Perfect One smiled, for the young monks were angry.

"Seven days will this excitement last, monks, and for that time only. But if they taunt you with that verse, reply with this.

> "The heroes, the Perfect Ones, lead by the Truth:—
> and who calls it amiss?
> If the Buddha persuades by the truth, will ye
> blame him for this?"

And the disciples smiled also and were content, and in seven days it was forgotten, and still the great and lowly flocked to hear.

Now of the people who flocked to him many desired signs and wonders that so they might be convinced of the truth, but these were not given in that manner and the Blessed One forbade his disciples to exalt themselves thus. For there is nothing but the taintless beauty of Law throughout the worlds, and the wise know there is no miracle at all, but only a higher law, not known to the ignorant, which in its action appears to them strange and a miracle. Yet did our Lord teach that for the instructed there are the powers, since to them in their higher consciousness the bonds of time and space and form exist no more. But it is useless and perilous to expose these mysteries before the ignorant who can but see in them the breaking of the law, and see it either with fear or greed. Therefore he taught that those who have attained should be wise and silent in knowledge where the occasion does not demand speech or action, and very rarely can they be demanded, for each stage has its own knowledge and cannot rise to the knowledge of a consciousness above its own. Hence all this foolish talk of miracle and the like. But for those who know even in part the fetters are broken :—the binding fetters of form, time and space. And of such a case the Lord told this story, while he rested at one time at Jetavana :

"There was a faithful, noble, joyful disciple who desired to hear again the words of Him who has thus Attained, and he came in the evening to the river Aciravati, hoping to cross by the ferry. But so it was that the boatman had himself gone to hear the great words and there was no ferry. Then, joyful in meditating on the light, and lost to all else, that faithful disciple walked on the water of the river, and his feet made no holes in the water, and he went as if on dry land. But suddenly in the middle of the river he saw waves, and his joy sank and his feet with it, for fear entered his soul and fear is a fetter of the world of form, so that he immediately became subject to it. But again he strengthened his inmost self in meditation on the Enlightened One, and again he walked on the water and so came to Jetavana and saluted the Blessed One, and took his seat respectfully beside him, and the Lord asked ; "Disciple, did you come with little fatigue by the road? Have you lacked for food?" And he replied ;

"Lord, in my joyful meditation I received support

so that I walked on the water and did not sink, and thus have I come to Jetavana as though I walked on dry land."

And the Lord said; "So also has it been in past lives."

For he taught that though there are times and seasons for the powers to be manifested to the ignorant, they are very few.

## CHAPTER XIV

Now while the Perfect One dwelt by Rajagriha there came to him a message from Kapila, from his father, the Maharaja Suddhodana, and it said this :

" My son, tidings have reached me of great things concerning you and the fulfilment of prophecies. But of these I will not speak for it is fitting that I should hear them from your own lips. But this I have to say : Is it not just and right that I should see my son before I die ? Come to me."

And when this reached the Enlightened One it was impossible that he should doubt or hesitate, for who had more right to call upon him ? And so, preparing himself for the journey on foot with certain of his disciples, once more he set his face to Kapila looking toward the mountains.

And many things filled his heart, of memory and of affection, but all now controlled and guided by divine knowledge and certitude, so that he went surrounded by peace and glad in that he carried a great gift to his father exceeding all gold, all jewels of all kings, if so it could be received, repaying thus the tenderness which had guarded his youth.

And when the Maharaja and the people of Kapila heard he would come, from that day forth they watched the ways to the city that they might with due eagerness and joy welcome the great return of their Prince. For they said proudly :

" Our Prince who left us to seek enlightenment has

now found it, and gloriously returns!" and they thought:

"To what kingdom has the like happened?"

So journeying on foot, the Blessed One, crowned with the Ten Perfections, at last approached Kapila, and those who were the far outposts of the watch ran back to the next and those to the next until it reached the city, crying:

"The Prince comes! The Prince comes!"

And the Maharaja having prepared himself, surrounded by his lords and all the neighbouring nobility, went forth along the flower-strewn ways (for the people hurried with flowers and banners and perfumes) to meet the great guest. And the heart of the Maharaja was hot within him and exulted, thinking:

"He returns and the clouds are past and the sun of his glory drowns all in its brightness, and my good days are come again."

So they paused in the principal street of the town and there waited in the shade, with banners and flowers making gay the blue air about them.

Then at long last moving through the streets, followed by two others, the Maharaja and his nobles saw a young monk clad in the yellow robe, with one shoulder bared, who in his hands carried an alms-bowl, and at each house door stopped and silently tendered the bowl, receiving with majesty what was given, and passing on with patience when it was refused. And it was his son.

Then shame and love and anger contended in the heart of the Maharaja and tore him like a whirlwind among the leaves of a tree, and he clenched his robe across his breast and cried out aloud to Siddhartha:

"I am put to shame—to horrible shame. My son a beggar! Our race is beaten to the earth with shame."

And standing calmly before the angry Maharaja the

Blessed One after due salutation lifted his eyes and replied: "Maharaj, this is the custom of our race."

"This horrible thing is not so. Not one of our ancestors has ever begged his bread."

"Maharaj, you and your high race claim descent from kings,—but my descent is far otherwise. It is from the Buddhas of ancient days, and as they have done, begging their food from the charitable, so do I, nor can I otherwise."

But seeing his father still in pain from anger and sorrow, the Perfected One spoke thus:

"Do I not know that the King's heart bleeds with love and memory, and that for his son's sake he adds grief to grief? But now let these earthly bonds of love be instantly unloosened and utterly destroyed, for there are greater and higher. Ceasing from thought of such love, let the King's mind receive from me such spiritual food as no son has yet offered to father, a gift most beautiful and wonderful."

So leading the King by the hand they went together to the palace, the mind of the Maharaja quieted and subdued as after a storm the billows sink to rest.

And within the palace the Perfected One looked for another, but she was not there, for her very life beat against her body in agony, remembering, remembering, and she said in her heart;

"I will not go. I cannot go. If I am of any value in his eyes, I, the mother of his son, he will come to me. I cannot go to him."

So, when a little time had passed, the Perfected One arose, and attended by the two mightiest of his disciples and followed by the Maharaja went to the Palace of his wife, and as he went, he said:

"Monks, if this lady should embrace me, do not hinder her, though it be against the rule."

And pacing silently beside him, the two comprehended the wisdom and compassion of the Lord, bowing their heads.

And they entered the hall where the Princess stood unveiled, the glory of her hair shorn, clad in a coarse robe of yellow resembling his own, and divested of all jewels and splendours, and she stood like the marble image of a woman as he entered, pale in the shadows.

Then, seeing him, suddenly love and manifold anguish broke in a freshet in her heart as when the melting snows fill Rohini until she floods her banks; and pride and love, each stabbed to the heart, strove within her, and with piteous eyes she looked upon her Lord, once so near and now so far, as he stood calmly regarding her with a look she could not understand, and love had the victory, and she ran to him and falling on the ground laid her face upon his feet and embraced them weeping most bitterly.

And there was silence, none hindering or speaking, and he looked down upon her.

So she lay.

But after awhile remembrance returned to her and his silence and the distance wide as heaven and earth between them, and she rose with majesty and withdrew herself to one side and stood with bowed head while the Maharaja declared to the Perfected One her griefs and patience and mortifications so that she might resemble him, abjuring her bed for a mat laid upon the ground, and the feasts of the palace for one poor meal a day, and much more. And the Prince heard and speaking slowly, still with his eyes upon her, said:

"This is true. Great also was the virtue of this high lady, the mother of Rahula, virtue in a former life which I remember and she too will remember one day with gladness. Lady, mother of my son, the way that I have opened is open for you also. Come and hear."

And with his eyes upon her to the last he turned and went away.

So that evening, seated by the bank of Rohini, the Perfect One taught the Way before his own people, and they crowded to hear: and this high lady seated, veiled so that none might see her hidden eyes, heard also, and as she listened, illusion fell from her; she perceived the Unchanging, the Formless, the Beautiful, and the illusory forms of this world and the delusion of time fell from her also, and she beheld her love no longer past and done with, but eternal as the eternity of the Self that alone endures, and the imprisoning self which alone can suffer died within her and left her enfranchised, and inward light shone upon her and she knew the truth.

So also was it with the Maharaja and the Maharani Prajapati and many more.

But on the next day the Princess Yashodara called to her son Rahula and dressed him in his best until he shone bright and beautiful as a star, and she laid her cheek against his, saying:

"Go now, beloved, and seek your father and ask for your inheritance."

And he answered:

"Mother, I know of no father but the Maharaja. What father? And why should he withhold my inheritance?"

And she said: "Go and ask. But first see, that you may know him."

She led the boy to the window and pointed.

"That monk, clothed in the yellow robe, he whose face shines like the sun in its strength, is your father. And he has great wealth—riches not to be told in words. Go, son, and demand your inheritance."

And the boy went, wondering and desiring, and in the garden he ran quickly and catching the robe of the Blessed One, he said:

"My father, how happy I am to be near you. O day of gladness," and tears of joy overflowed his eyes, seeing his father so great and beautiful, But to test him, the Blessed One was silent, pacing toward the Nyagrodha grove, and still the child followed, entreating for his inheritance.

Then when they reached the grove, the Perfected One turned smiling to Sariputta the great disciple, and he said:

"Monk, what think you? For worldly wealth perishes, but this remains. Shall I make my son heir to the Greatest? Let us admit him to the Order."

And it was done, and the heart of the Princess sang within her for bliss, and henceforward the boy trod the way of Peace.

So leaving joy and tranquillity behind him and measureless content in the soul of Yashodara, the Blessed One returned to Shravasti on the river Rapti, and there a rich merchant, Anathapindika, gave to the Order a pleasant grove named Jetavana, and a monastery, and there during the rains our Lord dwelt and many of his teachings and discourses were spoken at Jetavana.

And this was the manner of his life.

The Blessed One would rise early in the morning, and that some one of his followers might gain merit he accepted service, and water was brought to him for ablution, and having performed this he would sit alone until it was time to go and beg his food. Then he would put on his tunic, girdle, and robe, and taking his bowl would enter the village or town for alms. Sometimes alone, sometimes with other monks, many of them men of great and noble birth. And it seemed that gentle breezes cleared the air for him and clouds let fall rain to lay the dust, and where he placed his foot the way was even and pleasant and flowers blossomed. And it appeared to those who saw, that rays of radiance surrounded his person, since he possessed the attributes of that true world which encompasses the illusions of the false world perceived by the senses.

By all these tokens and more did the people know who approached, and they said to each other:

"Bhagavat—the Blessed One—has now entered for alms," and robed in their best, with perfumes, flowers, and such offerings as they could give, they came into the street. There, having paid their homage, some would implore him.

"Reverend sir, let us feed ten monks," and some, "Let us feed twenty," and the rich "Let us feed a hundred." And the most fortunate would take the bowl of the Blessed One and fill it with food.

When he had finished his meal, the Blessed One considering what was suited to the minds of those who listened, would so teach them the Law that many would attain to the fruit of knowledge in its different degrees, and some in the highest—that of a clear perception in saintship,—and having thus given his good gifts to the multitude he would rise and return to the quiet monastery.

On his arrival there he sat in a pavilion shaded from the sun, on an excellent Buddha-mat which had been spread for him, and there waited for the monks to finish their meal, and when this was done he entered his chamber and bathed his feet from the dust of travel.

Then, standing, he exhorted the assembly of monks, saying:

"Monks, diligently work out your salvation, for not often is a Buddha—an Enlightened One—seen in the world—not often is it possible thus to hear the Law. And if even an animal can keep the Precepts, how much more a man."

And at this point some would ask the Blessed One for exercises in meditation and to each he assigned what suited best their characters. And then all did obeisance to the Perfect One, and dispersed to the places where they were in the habit of spending the night or day, some to the forest, some to the foot of trees, some, in meditation, to the heavenly places.

And the Blessed One, then entering his chamber, would, if wearied, lie down for awhile, not sleeping but mindful and conscious and on his right side, as a lion takes his repose. And when refreshed he rose, and sent his gaze through the world (for to the Illuminated this is possible), to see who it was possible he might aid.

And after this, the people of the village or town near which he might be dwelling assembled, again in their best robes, and he, approaching with majesty, took his seat on the Buddha-mat in the little audience hall, and declared the doctrine to his hearers who sat before him rapt in hearing.

And when they had made obeisance and departed it was the custom of the Perfected One to bathe himself, and after that to assume his tunic and girdle, and throwing his robe over his right shoulder to go into his chamber and there fall into deep meditation, and after that was the rest of the day given to the monks who assembled, coming from here, there, and everywhere, to question the Blessed Lord and ask his instructions or plead for a sermon, and all this he very gladly gave, so consuming the first watch of the night.

And during the middle watch of the night he would commune with the blessed spirits of the Universe, they drawing very near him in the true accord.

And the last watch of the night he divided into three parts, and weary with much sitting he paced up and down considering many things, and in the second part would enter his chamber and rest, and in the third, seated, send the diamond-clear ray of his perception through the world that he might commune with any soul who needed that communion.

And thus were spent the days of him who had attained the *Paramitas*, the Ten Perfections.

And if there be any who would know of the ten, these are they.

Almsgiving, morality, long-suffering, manliness, meditation, mystic insight, resolution, strength, knowledge, and skill in the choice of means.

In all these was our Lord perfected. And above even these in Love. For hear the teaching of the Lord:

"As a mother, even at the risk of her own life, protects her son, her only son, so let the disciple cultivate love without measure toward all beings. Let him cultivate toward the whole world above, below, around, a heart of love unstinted, unmixed with differing or opposing interests. And let a man maintain this mindful love whether he stands, walks, sits or lies. For in all the world this state of heart is best."

For the Lord, the Blessed One, taught that this love must increase until the wide Universe is suffused with its radiance.

"Our mind shall not waver. No evil speech will we utter. Tender and compassionate will we abide, loving, void of malice. And with rays of love shall we suffuse all that is, even with love grown great and measureless."

And because of this high teaching many men and women attained to Arhatship, becoming perfected saints, seeing things as they are in themselves and not according to their illusory appearances in this world of illusion,—and they made great songs of triumph and victory, saying that when the Hindrances are removed from a man he is as one set free from debt, imprisonment, and slavery.

"For when the five Hindrances are put away within him, he is a free man and secure, and gladness springs up within him, and joy, and so rejoicing all his frame becomes at ease, and in that peace his heart is stayed."

And again, this song of Right Rapture.

> " It is in very bliss we dwell, we who
> hate not those who hate us :
> Among men full of hate we dwell, who
> are void of hate.
> It is in very bliss we dwell, we in health
> among the ailing.
> Among men weary and sick, we continue well.
> It is in very bliss we dwell, we, free from care
> among the careworn.
> Among men tortured with unrest, we are calm.
> It is in very bliss we dwell, we who have no
> hindrances.
> We have become feeders on joy, like to the
> shining Gods."

" The shining Gods." What then are these Gods and Shining Ones ? Thus have I heard.

Surely the Gods are they who having acquired mighty merit by great good deeds reign and shine for ages until the power of their good deeds is exhausted. For they knew not the Nirvana and the disintegration of the false self, and so desired Paradise as their reward, and Paradise they have. But though it last for ages, when the power of their good deeds is exhausted then they too must enter again by the gate of birth and humbly learn to extinguish all desire, even though it be the desire of Heaven, and to know that the greedy *I* which desired these things is non-existent, until they too, treading the Noble Eightfold Path, enter upon the highest wisdom and attain to the Nirvana, the Peace, for this alone is that comprehension which beholds the heavens and hells as pictures, as illusions, as nothing,—and whoso possesses it sits above manhood and Godhead alike, having utterly attained.

Thus it must be when ignorance is dead and wisdom made perfect, for the vain shows of ignorance are dispersed in clear perception of the things that are true and eternal.

When the wise man by earnestness has driven vanity far away, he has climbed the terraced heights of wisdom, and, care-free, looks down upon the illusory world, the careworn crowd, as he who standing upon a mountain top watches serenely the toilers in the plain.

And a man must have what he desires, be it the Paradises that pass, or the Peace that is eternal.

## CHAPTER XV

THUS have I heard:

Now persons of all castes, high and low, women as well as men, sought the teachings of the Lord—and he received all with courtesy and gladness, for he said:

"There is no caste in blood and tears."

So they brought him their griefs and questionings. And very strange to them did it seem to behold a great Prince surrounded by young men of the noble families who each and all had thrown off the Hindrances of the illusory world and forsaking all had followed the Truth.

But when they themselves had seen the light no longer did it appear strange, for who will stay to watch a fragment of broken glass flash in the sun, when before him pulse the great lights of a royal jewel, brother of the sun and stars.

And about this time the beautiful harlot of Vaisali, the Lady Amra, lovely as the divine Shri rising from the ocean, heard that a great Lord of Wisdom was come to Vaisali, and she offered him the use of her Garden of Mangoes outside the city that he might rest in the delicious shade of her trees and in the little pavilion where she took her pleasure, for she was rich in gold and jewels and resembled a great Princess in pride and beauty. But she did not herself think to see him, for the joy of life held her as the nectar of flowers holds the clinging bee, making his wings heavy so that he scarce can fly.

But her steward came to her, saying:

"O auspicious lady, I know not how it is, but all the nobles and people are afoot, making their way to the Garden of Mangoes, and when I asked the reason they replied:

"It is because of the man who rests there. There is none like him—none! And he is the son of a King and has forsaken his kingdom that he may find a greater."

And she leaped to her feet laughing, ever ready for some new sight, saying:

"Is it so? Then make ready my vehicle and I will go with Subaddha to see the man."

And they harnessed her velvet-white oxen with tassels of gold to her gilded car, and she took her place with the lady Subaddha at her feet and a golden canopy above her head, shining like the moon in her glory, and she went as a queen, casting proud glances about her.

Now it was so early in the day that folk were busied with their labours and the nobles were yet sleeping and the way was clear before her, and the oxen trod quietly between the neem trees and fan palms until she came to the gate of her Garden of Mangoes, and there they halted in young sunlight and the dew of dawn. And a man stood by the gate as though he guarded it, and he was robed in yellow with one arm and shoulder bare, and when she would have entered he stretched out his arm and forbade her, saying:

"Lady, being such a woman as you are, how is it seemly that you should enter this garden? Return whence you came."

And the blood fell away from her face and left her pale at that saying, for she had lived all her life like a queen, and now it seemed that scorn and the end were come upon her, and her beauty nothing though she shone like a night of moon and stars in her woven webs of gold. And silence fell upon her as she looked upon this noble young man serene and beautiful, who regarded her not, nor could she say, " The garden is mine," for she was afraid.

So then, between the feathering palms and the bamboo leaves that floated on still air, came another man, also clothed in the yellow robe, but walking like a Prince, and he said softly to the other :

" Stay her not, brother Yasas, for our Master would look upon her beauty. Descend, Lady, and follow."

And a little comforted at his saying she descended from beneath the canopy and followed through the palms and the mango trees that were her own and now seemed not hers. And there was great quiet, for the monk said no word and the leaves forbore to stir and not a cricket chirped and the sun was very early and dewy in the green ways. And she thought :

" What shall I see ? For kings and princes have feared my beauty and I mocked them. And if he be wise, yet have the stern ascetics of the forests—those whose power the very Gods dreaded,—been seduced from their wisdom by the nymphs of Heaven. They have gone utterly astray, and very certainly I am beautiful as Menaka or Urvasi."

And now they turned into a green way beside the still pool where the lotuses bloomed, and it was cool and dim with a deep shade of trees, for they let down pillared stems to root again in earth and make a forest temple that scarcely a ray might pierce. And within the shade was One seated with folded hands and feet and behind his head a raying light that shone like the midnight moon, and, lost in calm, he looked out into the worlds.

And the man beside her fell on his knees and hid his face.

Not for me, O, not for me, least of all the disciples is it meet that I should tell of this or of the similitude of the Blessed One—the very wise, the passionless, the desireless Lord in the eyes of such as loved him. Only this I know, that the woman stood amazed, forgetting her beauty, forgetting herself, forgetting all in the Three Worlds but only that One. And the rock crystal that was her heart melted within her and flowed away in a river of tears: nor could she stay her feet, but slowly, very slowly, she approached and before his feet she fell and laid her face on the earth.

Now after awhile the Exalted One commanded her to rise and be seated, and he incited and gladdened her with high discourse so that she could no longer fear but only love in hearing these great words with ears that drank them as the parched earth yearns for the rains. And if it be asked how a woman of evil life should thus be honoured, should thus harken with love and understanding, I tell this thing.

Many lives ago was there a deep forest where beasts and birds dwelt and nourished their young in peace, but one day a wind blew and brought on its wings a great fire. And none had pity on the beasts and birds but one pheasant, glorious of plumage, and this, caring nothing for her own life plunged into a stream of pure water, and flying upward shook the drops from her feathers on the flames. Therefore Indra, King of the Gods, seeing said:

"Foolish bird! and what can this do? You weary yourself in vain! This is a deed for the great and not for a little bird!'"

And she: "You are Indra, King of Heaven, and with a wish you could quench this fire, yet do not. But as for me while it burns I have no time for words."

And again she flew against the fire, sprinkling water. And the Great God blew with his breath, extinguishing the fire, but the pheasant had perished. Now in that former life was the Lady Amra that bird, and because the fruit of a high deed can never perish, so, passing through many lives, she attained at last to lie at the feet of the Blessed One. Just and perfect is the Law.

So, seated, at his feet, she received the Heart of Wisdom and accepted the first noble Truth, the Truth of suffering. And when the Exalted One judged that she could receive no more that day, he dismissed her and she bowed at his feet and said this :

" O, may the Lord in deep compassion do me the honour of eating at my house to-morrow."

And all assembled thought this could not be, but the Blessed One gave by silence his consent, and circling reverently about him three times she departed glad of heart, and the people made way for one so honoured.

Now the nobles of Vaisali had come out to meet the World-Honoured and they were on the road, and Amra in the dancing joy of her heart drove up against them, axle to axle, and they said angrily.

" How is it, Amra, that you, being such a one, drive up against us ? "

And she cried aloud :

" Noble persons, I have bidden the Exalted One for to-morrow's meal, and he comes—he comes ! "

And they halted amazed, and said :

" Sell us the honour of his company for great weights of gold."

And she, glowing with joy :

" Noble persons, were you to give me Vaisali and all its subject territories yet would I not give up this honourable meal."

And the angry nobles cast up their hands, crying :

" We are outdone by this mango-girl ! We are out-reached by this mango-girl."

And in anger they proceeded to the garden and went in before the Lord where he sat surrounded with calm, and they said :

" May the Exalted One do us the honour of taking his meal together with his disciples at one house to-morrow ? "

But he replied.

"Noble persons, I have promised to eat with the Lady Amra."

And again they threw up their hands, exclaiming:

"We are outdone by this mango-girl. Great shame to us is this!"

And the Lord Buddha robed himself early in the morning and took his begging bowl and his disciples followed, and he went to the Street of Flowers, and Amra set sweet milk-rice and cakes before the Lord and his followers and she herself attended upon them in great humility and they ate the food they had not thought to eat, and when it was eaten, she sat lowly by his side and folding her hands, said:

"Holy One, I present this house to the Order. Accept it, if it be your will."

And the Blessed One accepted the gift, seeing the heart that made it, and after inciting and gladdening her with high discourse, he rose and went his way.

And in merciful deeds and right living this lady grew, and the Heart of Wisdom strengthened in her, and in this very life she became a perfected saint—a great Arhat—and entered the Nirvana—the Peace. For, as the lotus flowers do not grow on dry land but spring from black and watery mud, so even by the strength of her passion and sin and the deeps of experience she reached the heights. And she it was who made The Psalm of Old Age, and smiled in its making.

"Glossy and black as the down of the bee my curls once clustered.
They, with the waste of years, are liker to hemp or to bark cloth,
Such and not otherwise, runneth the rune of the Soothsayer.

Lovely the lines of my ears as the delicate work of
the goldsmith.
They, with the waste of years, are seamed with
wrinkles and pendent.
Such and not otherwise runneth the rune of the
Soothsayer.

Full and lovely in rounding rose of old the small
breasts of me.
They, with the waste of years, droop sunken as skins
without water.
So and not otherwise runneth the rune of the Sooth-
sayer.

Such hath this body been. Now age-weary, weak and
unsightly,
Home of manifold ills: old house whence the mortar
is dropping,
So and not otherwise runneth the rune of the Sooth-
sayer."[1]

And inasmuch as the Sister thus discerned impermanence in all phenomena, knowing the world we see is but the creation of our senses, she, making clear her insight, attained, leaving behind her all fear and grief. For who shall measure the bounds and deeps and height and length of that wisdom that is one with Love?

Hear also the story of the very wise and glad and gay Lady Visakha—that pillar of the Order, who abiding in the world as a great lady of riches yet gave her heart to wisdom and the Law of the Perfect One, for open is the way to all.

She was daughter to a great man, Balamitra, and was a young maiden in her father's house, when a Brahman

[1] Translated by C. F. Rhys Davids.

commissioned by the Treasurer Migara to choose a wife for his son came that way, and when he arrived he saw Visakha and other girls going into the wood in search of amusement, and he watched them idly.

Now the other girls were frivolous, running, skipping, whirling about and singing, but Visakha walked quietly with them, observing all and saying little. And when they came to the tank the others carelessly stripped themselves and began to play in the clear water. But Visakha lifted her clothes by degrees as she entered and by degrees lowered them as she came out, careful and modest in her conduct. And, after this, food was distributed, and the other girls ate hurriedly and greedily and then gave the remnants to their attendants. But Visakha gave food first to those who served her, and then ate temperately herself.

And the Brahman, still watching, saw that as the girls returned there was water across the path and the others took off their shoes and waded, but Visakha remained shod, and when they came to a wood she kept her sunshade up though the others lowered theirs.

And there the Brahman came up with her, in much astonishment and questioned her, and seeing him to be a holy and dignified person she replied with respectful courtesy. And thus he said:

"Dear girl, whose daughter are you?"

"Sir, I am the daughter of Balamitra."

"Dear girl, be not angry if I question you. While those girls were skipping, dancing and twirling, with other unseemly manners, you walked quietly. Why, dear girl?"

"Because, great sir, all girls are their parents' merchandise. If in leaping and twirling I were to injure myself, I must be kept by my parents while I live, for none would woo me."

"Good, dear girl. I understand. Now in entering

the water your companions stripped themselves but you went clothed and modest. And why ? "

" O uncle, maidens must be shame-faced. It is not well for them to be seen unclothed."

" Dear girl, there was none to see."

" Uncle, you saw."

" Good, dear girl ; and again, the others neglected their attendants, but you fed yours first. And why ? "

" For this reason, uncle ; we have easy days and feastful : they, hard work always."

" Good, dear girl. And why in wading through the water did you keep your shoes on ? "

" Because in water one cannot see where one plants one's feet. I would not cut mine ! "

" And in the wood, dear girl, you kept your sunshade open. Why ? For then there was shade from the trees ? "

" But also, uncle, the droppings of birds, the malice of the monkeys letting fall unpleasant fragments, the falling of leaves and twigs. In the open this seldom happens ; in a wood often.'"

So, full of delight at her good sense, the Brahman went to her parents, and asked her in marriage for the son of Migara. And he said :

" This girl will make a noble wife and a great lady, for she is full of thought for others and wise with the very wisdom of the Law. Give her to the son of Migara."

And it was granted and they sent her to her husband in the city of Savatthi. Now Visakha was one who followed the Enlightened One with all her wise heart, but it was not so with Migara, her husband's father, nor yet with his household. But she gratified their eyes for they demanded the Five Beauties in a daughter of the House, and these five she richly possessed, namely, beauty of hair, beauty of flesh, beauty of bone, beauty of skin, and beauty of youth.

And beauty of hair is when the hair resembles a peacock's tail, falling to the end of the tunic where it curls upward. Beauty of flesh, when the lips resemble a bright red gourd. Beauty of bone, when the teeth gleam between the rosy lips like cut mother-of-pearl, with even division. Beauty of skin, when without the application of any cosmetic it is smooth as a lotus wreath and white as Kanikara flowers. Beauty of youth is the endurance of the gaiety and freshness of youth after many child-births. All these had Visakha, and yet another, for her voice was sweeter than music, like the silver sounding of a little gong. And on parting her father presented her with a magnificent jewel adornment known as the Great Creeper Parure, and a part of it consisted of a peacock with five hundred feathers of red gold in each wing, the beak of coral, the eyes of jewels and likewise the neck and tail-feathers. And on Visakha's head it resembled a peacock perched on a height, and it gave forth music and appeared to be real.

But when she was established in her new home she found that Migara, her father-in-law, was a follower of the naked ascetics, and they and he cast scorn on the Perfect One, and this disturbed her much, and the ascetics said to Migara :

" O householder, you have introduced into your family an arrant misfortune breeder, a disciple of the monk Gotama. Expel her instantly."

" And that is not easy ! " thought Migara, " for she comes of a great family,—But I will take measures."

So he sat down and began to eat sweet rice-milk from a golden bowl, and Visakha stood before him, dutifully fanning him. And a holy mendicant entered with his begging-bowl for alms, but Migara made as though he did not see him, and ate on, keeping his head down.

" Pass on, reverend sir ! " said Visakha with courtesy.

"My father is eating stale food—it would not be agreeable to you."

And when she said this, Migara leaped to his feet and cried:

"Take away this food and drive the girl from the house. To think the slut should accuse *Me* of eating stale food, and at a time of festival!"

"Father!" said Visakha, with composed serenity. "I shall not easily leave the house. For I am no harlot picked up at some river bathing place, but a great lady. And my father foresaw such a case, and when I left commanded eight householders of this town to investigate any charge brought against me. Summon them now."

And Migara agreed joyfully, knowing what they must adjudge to such insolence.

Then they came—eight grave and wise men, and the story was told. And when it was heard:

"Dear girl," said the eldest householder, "is it as he says?"

"That is not as *I* say! For when my father-in-law ignored the monk I said, 'He is eating stale fare.' And I meant this. He is uselessly consuming the merit acquired in a former life instead of making fresh. Now, what fault was that?"

"None, dear girl. Our daughter speaks justly. Why are you angry with her, sir?"

"Sirs, granted that was no fault. But when she came to us her mother gave her ten admonitions of a hidden meaning, and I dislike them. First: 'The indoor fire is not to be taken out of doors.' Now you know it is the friendly custom to send fire to our neighbours."

"Is it as he says, dear girl?"

"Good sirs, this is the meaning: 'If you notice any fault in any of your new family, never tell it outside the house. For there is no worse fire than this.' Was this a fault in me?"

And Migara was ashamed and said:

"Sirs, I grant this. But she was also instructed thus: 'Outdoor fire must not be brought indoors.' It is the custom to accept fire if ours should go out, and therefore this was an unseemly instruction."

And seated in a row and consulting, the householders appointed their eldest to answer.

"Is it as he says, dear girl?"

"No, good sirs. The meaning is—'If any outside the house speak ill of any within, never repeat it within doors. For there is no fire like the tongue."

"Well and good, dear girl. And the rest?"

And she repeated:

"I was instructed. 'Give to him who gives and also to him who does not give,' and this means, 'Be liberal to needy relatives and friends whether they can repay you or no.' And again: 'Sit happily.' And this means—'When you see your father-in-law or his wife or your husband, you must rise and stand before them.' 'Eat happily.' This means—'They must be served by you before you eat yourself.' 'Wait upon the fire.' This signifies, 'These three must be looked upon as beautiful as a flame of fire or a royal serpent.' 'Reverence the household divinities.' This means that these three are your divinities indeed. 'Sleep happily.' This means 'You must not lie down to sleep till you have done all possible services for them.' All these rules, good sirs, I have kept. Now am I in fault?"

And Migara sat with downcast eyes and the eight said to him:

"Treasurer, is there any other sin in our daughter for she is clear of any wrong in all this?"

And he said:

"No. None." But Visakha then arose in just anger.

"Good sirs," she said, "it would not have been fitting that I should be dismissed, yet now I am found guiltless I will go. It is a good time."

And she ordered her many carriages and slaves to be made ready. But Migara implored her to remain with them, half in fear and half in shame. And when she refused he redoubled his entreaties, and asked her forgiveness earnestly. And she replied:

"Good sir, what there is to pardon I pardon cheerfully. But I am a daughter to a family which follows the Law of the Exalted One. If I can be allowed to attend upon the Assembly, then I will stay. Not otherwise."

And he replied:

"Dear girl, wait on your Assembly as you please."

And the end of the matter was that Migara went with Visakha to hear the World-Honoured, doubtful and unwilling, and it appeared to Migara, as it did always to all, that the eyes of the Buddha were fixed steadfastly on him and his proclamation of the Law addressed to him, and to him only. And Migara heard and the words reached his innermost being and he became established in the truth and acquired an immovable faith in the Three Refuges—the Law, the Lord, and the Assembly. And he said:

"Truly it was for my advantage, truly it was for my good that my daughter-in-law came to my house," and when he returned, he touched her breast with his hand, saying:

"Henceforth you are as my mother," thus giving her the position of honour. And he caused to be made for her an ornament known as the Highly Polished Parure, and gave it to her under the eyes of the Buddha.

And she continued to give alms and to do many deeds of merit, and as the crescent moon rounds in the sky she became great in sons and daughters, ten of each. She lived to be an hundred and twenty years old, and not one gray hair was seen upon her head, insomuch that when she walked to the monastery with her children and their children, people asked:

"Which is the great Visakha?"

And they said. "That great lady who walks so lightly," and the others replied;

"May she walk further! Our lady looks well when she walks."

And those who saw her stand, sit, or lie, would say:

"I hope she may do each a little longer. Our lady looks well in all she does."

So that it could not be charged against her that there was any posture in which she did not look well.

And great and magnificent were her charities to all who needed. And even the great Creeper Parure she gave for the needy, and redeemed it with a King's ransom, and she attended upon the sick, healing them with wise medicaments, and she built a monastery, and it is easy to rehearse what she did not do that was good, but impossible to rehearse all her innumerable nobilities of deed and thought.

And it was of her the One who is Awakened said:

"Just, monks, as a skilful garland-maker if he obtain a heap of flowers will go on making beautiful garlands without end, even so does the mind of Visakha incline to do all manner of noble deeds weaving them into loveliness."

And this is the history of that great, generous and happy lady, the daughter of the Law, known henceforth as the mother of Migara who was the father of her husband.

## CHAPTER XVI

THUS have I heard:

At this time the Queen Prajapati, she who had nourished the Blessed One with noble milk when his mother Maya was received into Paradise, sent to our Lord, with a message from herself and from the Princess Yashodara and other ladies of the royal family, and it was this.

"Full of hindrances is the household life, very free the life of the homeless for such as would walk in the way. Let the Blessed One, the Happy One, permit that women also retire to the peace of the homeless life under the discipline taught by the Exalted Lord."

But he was silent, and a second time they made their petition, for they thought:

"Much need have women of the Peace, and is the way closed to them only?"

And the Queen Prajapati came herself and besought him with tears, and he replied:

"Enough, Lady. Do not make this request," and weeping and saluting him with reverence she left him.

So wandering from place to place and teaching by the way, the Blessed One came to Vaisali and stayed awhile in the Pagoda Hall, and when she knew where she could find him the Queen Prajapati with shorn hair and yellow robes, followed by a number of the Sakya women, journeyed along the dusty ways to Vaisali and stood in the porch of the Pagoda Hall weeping and very sorrowful.

Now it so chanced that the disciple Ananda, cousin

of the Exalted One and much loved by him (and he was chosen to wait always about his person), saw those weeping women stand in the porch, dusty and foreworn with the long journey and their tender feet swollen and cut with unwonted travel, and he pitied them and inquired into the cause of their grief.

And having heard all he approached the Blessed One with reverence where he sat full of peace looking out into the green shade of the nyagrodha trees, and after salutation Ananda the beloved sat down beside him waiting until the Lord turned his eyes serenely upon him. And then said Ananda:

"Reverend Sir, here in the entrance stands Prajapati the Queen with swollen feet, sorrowful and weeping, and her word is that the Blessed One will not permit women to retire to the homeless life. Exalted One, I beseech you for these. Let their petition be heard."

But the Blessed One replied:

"Enough, Ananda. Do not ask this."

And again and yet again the beloved Ananda besought and still the Lord refused. And then the thought occurred to Ananda that he might ask in another manner with more success, for he pitied the women for this great denial of their hope. And he said:

"Lord, if women retire to the homeless life is it possible for them to attain to the goal of returning only once more to rebirth? Is it possible that escaping from sorrow they should attain to saintship?"

And the Blessed One in whom is all truth, answered:

"This is possible."

And the face of Ananda gladdened even like his name which signifies Joy, and he said:

"Then I beseech the Perfected One to consider how great a benefactress to the Order has been the Queen. She is sister to the mother of the Blessed One and at her breast was he nourished. I beseech and yet again beseech that they be admitted, for if it be possible that they thus make an end of sorrow shall not this be permitted ? "

Then said the Blessed One :

" Hard is it to refuse and I cannot. If therefore these women will accept eight weighty regulations in addition to those accepted by the Order—eight weighty regulations making them subject to the Order, it shall be reckoned to them for ordination."

And when he had received the eight weighty regulations hard to be borne, for they set the oldest and most venerable of nuns below the youngest and least of the Order, Ananda went out to the Queen and told her all as she stood patiently with the wearied women. And when they heard the regulations sorrow passed from them as when the moon escaping from a cloud floats in pure radiance in pure air, and the Queen answered for Yashodara and for all those tender ones :

" Reverend Ananda, as a woman young, beautiful, and loving to beautify herself, having obtained a wreath of blue lotus-flowers, or of perfumed jasmin, takes it and wreathes her head with joy, so do we. O venerable Ananda, we take up those eight weighty regulations, not to be transgressed while life lasts."

And that was their ordination, as the Exalted One had said, and Ananda returned to the Lord and told him of their joy. And he meditated and said :

" If, Ananda, women had not retired to the homeless life, under my discipline then would religion have endured long in this country, even a thousand years. But now, not very long will the discipline and religion endure. And just as a man prudently builds a dike in order that water confined may not transgress its bounds, have I laid down the eight weighty regulations. Yet it shall not endure, since women have accepted the rules."

And true it is that in India the faith has not endured, but over the rest of Asia has it spread, strong and mighty.

But the women were glad at heart, for the homeless life drew them with the very passion of peace and many became great saints, some dwelling in forests and in caves, and great to them was the joy of peace in the solitudes far from crowds, and they were filled with the life of trees and great forests and the strength of the up-running sap and the speechless communion and growth of trees and plants. And in many joy broke forth in words and they made the Psalms of the Sisters, even as their brothers the monks also sang for joy and could no more be silent than birds at dawn, for the world they had known called to ears that heard no longer. And thus it called;

"Young art thou, sister, and faultless—what seekest
*thou* in the holy life?
Cast off that yellow-hued raiment and come!"

And each replied in her own manner.

"I what was well to do have done, and what
Is to my heart delectable. Therein
Is my delight, and thus through happiness
Has happiness been sought after and won."

Young and old they rejoiced, and the solitudes were kind to them, admitting them to fellowship. And one aged sister spoke this:

"Though I be suffering and weak and all
My spring of youth be gone, yet have I come
Leaning upon my staff and climbed aloft
On mountain peak. My cloak have I thrown off

My little bowl o'er-turned; so sit I here
Upon the rock. And o'er my spirit sweeps
The breath of Liberty. I win, I win
The Triple Lore! The Buddha's will be done."

For now, they who had been the prisoners of man and of opinion learnt the beauty of the solitudes, and knew the silence that is in the starry sky, the sleep that is among the lonely hills, and it became theirs, and they attained to the coolness, purity and luminance of the Peace, bathing in it as in moonlit water. For they had passed through the Three Grades of Training, the Higher Habit of Conduct, the Higher Consciousness, and the Higher Wisdom, and thus, knowing the world, not as it appears to be but as it is, knowing "This is Ill; this is the cause of Ill; this is the way leading to the cessation of Ill," they were glad, and right ecstasy was theirs and joys that cannot be told, and they were free.

And another said this:

"Nirvana have I realised and gazed
Into the mirror of the holy Norm.
I, even I, am healed of all my hurt.
Down is my burden laid, my task is done,
My heart is wholly set at liberty."

And again:

"One day bathing my feet, I sit and watch
The water as it trickles down the slope.
Thereby I set my heart in steadfastness,
As one shall train a horse of noble breed.
Then, going to my cell, I take my lamp,
And seated on my couch I watch the flame.

Taking the pin I pull the wick right down
Into the oil. Extinguished is the fire.
Lo, the Nirvana of the little lamp.
Emancipation dawns. My heart is free."

For as the flame is quenched so are all lusts, desires and cravings extinguished in the clear waters of Nirvana. There is no fire so burning as the greed of passion, no luckless cast of the dice so cruel as hate, no ill so miserable as that of the ego that would claim all. Nor is there any bliss to be compared with the Nirvana.

And the monks, also musing, made psalms that cannot die, for upon them also was the bliss.

"When in the lowering sky thunders the storm-cloud's drum,
And all the pathways of the birds are thick with rain,
The brother sits within the hollow of the hills
Alone, rapt in thought's ecstasy. No higher bliss
Is given to men than this.

Or where by rivers flowers crowd the bank,
And fragrant rushes scent the tranquil air,
With heart serene the brother sits to see,
Alone, rapt in an ecstasy. No higher bliss
Is given to men than this."

And another:

"Whene'er I see the crane, her clear pale wings
Outstretched in fear to flee the black storm cloud,
A shelter seeking, to safe shelter borne,
Then does the river Ajakarani
Give joy to me.

"Who shall not love to see on either bank
Clustered rose-apple trees in bright array
Beyond the great cave of the hermitage?
Or hear the soft croak of the frogs, their foes,
The legions of the air, withdrawn, proclaim
Now from the mountain streams is't time to-day
To flit. Safe is the Ajakarani.
She brings us luck! Here it is good to be."

Thus very great joy had come to be by the Blessed One's sufferings, and for each pang he had paid came a golden harvest of the peace of others.

To Him who had thus Attained came men and women from far and near with doubts and questions, and seated with dignity (for his noble Aryan birth was upon him as well as the Peace) he received them all, answering and resolving their doubts, nor was it difficult for him to do this for his eyes were as the sun in his strength to divide light from darkness.

Yet let it be well understood that of certain things he would not speak, counting them beyond human knowledge and knowing well that in no human speech are there words to bear the burden of the Ineffable. Therefore when men asked him of the Beginning, how division from the Eternal into the false ego-self came into the world and from what well of bitterness evil thought and evil doing flowed to become tears and blood in their flowing he would not answer, for none but a Buddha can comprehend the deepest, and he only in ways beyond transmission to others. And he would say:

"The arrow sticks in the wound, will you wait before the healer draws it out to inquire of what wood is it made and whether the bowstring is of hair or vegetable fibre? Life is ebbing while you theorise credulously

[1] These Psalms are all translated by C. F. Rhys Davids.

about present and future, self or identity. Of the origins I do not teach."

And when again they besought him to say whether life or nothingness lay beyond death, only his own nearest disciples could read the fathomless depths of his calm, looking rather to this than to his speech. For he said, being alone with them to whom it was given to know:

" In this world of forms and illusions created by our senses, according to our illusion a man either is or is not, either lives or dies, but in the true and formless world this is not so for all is otherwise than according to our knowledge and it is easier to answer in negatives than in affirmatives. And if you ask Does a man live beyond death, I answer No, not in any sense comprehensible to the mind of man which itself dies at death. And if you ask does a man altogether die at death, I answer No, for what dies is what belongs to this world of form and illusion, that is the false I, but beyond this is another world incomprehensible as yet to such as are not instructed and beyond all human categories, so that if I would I cannot tell you of it, but I would not, for the things are disturbing and do not aid the traveller on the only path which can bring him to their threshold. Therefore of that and of the origins I do not teach."

But this ego which the unenlightened believes to be himself, very certainly falls apart and dissolves at death, not is there any place of continuance for it, and it is wholly extinct.

And it so happened that one day a wandering monk, by name Vacchagotta, came to the Exalted One, and saluting him with friendly greetings he sat down beside him, and he asked.

" How does the matter stand, venerated Gotama? In a man is there the Ego? "

And the Exalted One was silent, and Vacchagotta

asked again and yet again and still there was silence, and after a while he rose and went away.

But the beloved Ananda came to Him who has thus Attained, and said:

"Why, sir, did you not answer the wandering monk Vacchagotta?" And, smiling, he looked in the face of the beloved Ananda.

"If, Ananda, when he asked me, I had answered 'The ego is,' then that reply would have confirmed the teaching of those who believe in the permanence of that false ego which is a bundle of tendencies and consciousness and proudly calls itself I and the Soul; and if I had said the ego is not, this would have confirmed the teaching of those who say there is annihilation and nothing beyond death. For neither of these schools, nor yet Vacchagotta, know the distinction between the ego of which he asked me and the true Ego, for this last is eternal and beyond comprehension, and the false ego passes and is gone like a dream in the awakening of dawn. Therefore since Vacchagotta has not attained to the threshold of that knowledge, being prisoned in the world of appearances, what could I do but keep silence?"

And the beloved Ananda laid his hand upon his mouth and retired, for with all his heart of love he had not yet attained to the full insight of the unreality of appearances, but where he could not understand he loved. And love is also the Way, as witness the monk Purna who was about to carry the light into a land of violent and perilous people. So the Perfected One sent for him, and asked:

"And if, monk, these people abuse and injure you, what will be your thought?"

"That these people are good in that they only abuse me and do not beat me."

"But if they beat you?"

"Then I shall think they are good in that they only beat me and do not stab me with swords."

"But if with swords?"

"Then I shall think: They are good. They leave me my life."

"But if they take your life?"

"Then,—They are good to me in that they have lifted a burden from me."

And looking upon his face the World-Honoured said:

"Well have you spoken, Purna, Go and deliver, you who have delivered yourself. Comfort, for you are comforted. Guide to the Peace, for you have entered it."

So Purna went in joy.

And there was a monk named Yamaka who, considering the teaching, believed that on the dissolution of the body the man who has lost all depravity is annihilated and exists no more. And his fellow monks having in vain urged him to abandon so wicked a heresy called upon Sariputta the Great to teach him better, and by his silence he consented.

So when the evening was come, Sariputta the Great rose from deep meditation and drawing near to Yamaka he greeted him with courtesy as one monk should another and sitting down respectfully beside him he questioned him thus:

"Is the report true, brother Yamaka, that the wicked heresy of annihilation has sprung up in your mind?"

"Even so, brother, do I understand the teaching of the Blessed One."

And Sariputta the Great mused a moment and resumed:

"What think you, brother Yamaka;—is his bodily form the saint?"

"No indeed, brother."

"Are sensation, perception, predispositions, the saint?"

"Certainly not, brother."

"Then can you consider the saint as apart and distinct from form, sensation, perception and predispositions?"

"Brother, I cannot."

"And if separately they are not, are they when united the saint?"

"Brother, no."

"Then what think you, brother Yamaka? If you cannot prove the very existence of the saint in this world of forms and appearances, is it reasonable for you to say that at death the saint is annihilated and does not exist."

And holding down his head for shame Yamaka answered.

"Brother Sariputta, it was through ignorance I held that wicked heresy, but now I have acquired the True Doctrine."

For Sariputta the Great taught as did his Master that the true being is detached from each of these delusive selves of consciousness, sensation, perception, and predispositions, and the saint who has attained has detached himself even in this life from belief that these are himself—his ego. How then should it be that the essential perishes when these dissolve with the dying brain in death? Yet has this wicked heresy been spread, though clear as day must it be made to those who tread the way that it is a lie and no truth.

For thus have I heard. After the death of the Perfected One, the King of Kosala, journeying from Savatthi, met with the learned nun Khema, renowned for wisdom, and the King, respectfully saluting her, asked her of the Teaching.

"Venerable Lady, the Perfect One is dead. Does he exist after death?"

"Great King, the Exalted One has not declared that he exists after death."

"Then, venerable Lady, does the Perfect One not exist."

"The Perfect One has not declared that he does not exist after death."

"But, venerable Lady,—does and does not? How is this possible?"

And, smiling a little, the learned nun replied.

"Great King, have you an accountant or a mint-master who could count the sands of Ganges and lay the figure before you?"

"Venerable Lady, no."

"Or who could measure the drops in the ocean?"

"Again no, venerable Lady."

"And why? Because the ocean is deep, immeasurable, unfathomable. So also is it if the existence of the Perfect One be measured by any human category, for all statements of bodily form are abolished in the Perfect One; their root is severed; they are done with and can germinate no more. The Perfect One is released from the possibility that his being can be gauged in any human terms. He is now deep, immeasurable and unfathomable as the ocean, and neither the terms of existence or of non-existence as understood by the world fit him any more."

Then there was a long silence and the King, having heard the nun Khema's words with approbation, rose and bowed reverently before her and went his way.

Eye hath not seen, nor ear heard, nor can the tongue tell of such matters for they are beyond and above us. And it is for this reason that the Blessed One replied thus to the venerable Malukya, when he reproached the Perfect One as follows:

"Is the world eternal or the slave of time? Does the World-Honoured live on beyond death? It pleases me not at all that all these important matters should remain unanswered. May it please the Master to answer them if he can. And if he does not know let him say so plainly."

But the Master replied with his smile:

"Did I say to you, Malukya,—'Come and be my disciple, and I will teach you whether the world is everlasting or infinite, whether the vital faculty is separate from the body or one with it, whether the Exalted One lives or does not live after death?' Did I promise all this?"

"No, sir, you did not."

"And, Malukya, if a man is struck by a poisoned arrow, suppose he says—'I will never allow my wound to be treated until I know who shot the arrow—was it a man of high or low caste. And I must know whether he is tall or short, and how his bow and arrows are made!' —Would this be a sensible proceeding? Surely no. He would die of his wounds.

"Why have I not made these things clear? Because the knowledge of them does not conduce to holiness nor right detachment, nor to peace and enlightenment.—What is needed for these I teach, the truth of suffering and its origin, the truth of the Way to its cessation. Therefore let what I have not revealed rest, and follow that which I have revealed."

And Malukya was content, knowing at last that in this life these questions are deep, mysterious and unanswerable, and the sole way to their understanding is to live the life, untroubled by controversy and dogma on such things as cannot be uttered in terms of human knowledge.

For there is a Knowledge veiled in excess of light which dazzles the eyes to blindness. Let words be few. Let good deeds be many. He understands it for whom it passes thought. Who thinks of it can never know it. And if it could be told in words it would not be the Truth.

And there is yet another example of this. For once

in early days the Blessed One sat high among his own upon the Peak of Vultures, and there came before his quiet feet a Shining One and laid there a golden flower, praying that he would speak and in sweet speech instruct them of the innermost of the Peace. The Blessed One received the golden flower within his hand and sat in utter calm but spoke no word and all the Assembly mused what this might mean, and, musing, could not know. But at long last, Kassapa the Great smiled, also in silence, and the Blessed One said softly:

"I hold within my heart the Treasure of the Law, the wondrous knowledge that is the Peace. This have I given to Kassapa wordless, and wordless he has seen and known.'"

So passes the vision from heart to heart. But words cannot tell it to the brain.

# CHAPTER XVII

THUS have I heard:

A Brahman, high and haughty, having great possessions and full of this world's power, raised his voice railing against the teaching of the Holy One, saying:

"But this is against the teaching of the Vedanta! Who shall hear Gotama the Sakya when he teaches thus?"

And he came proudly from Rajagriha far off, and stood beside to hear, that he might scoff at his ease, but the nobleness of the teacher drew him as with the kindred understanding of high birth, and the marvellous deeps of the Law caught him by the pride of his intellect for he thought it was too high for the foolish, and the wisdom beyond all words that falls like dew on the thirsty soul subdued him into an amazing quiet, and when it was done he went alone into the wood and sat himself in the shade by a clear running stream and considered these things in his heart.

But he could not stay away for cords drew him and bonds were forged between him and That Other and they were smithied in iron unbreakable. So after awhile he rose, and hanging his head went back to the Jetavana monastery and demanded to see the World-Honoured, and when he came, this Brahman Vasettha made due salutation and seated himself respectfully beside him, and he said:

"It has been told to me, Gotama, that the monk Gotama knows the way to the state of union with the Ultimate."

And the Perfect One replied:

"What is to be known I know."

"So has it been told to me, Gotama. It is well. Let the venerable Gotama be pleased to show me the way."

Then said the Happy One:

"Know, Vasettha, that from time to time is born into the world a fully Enlightened One happy with knowledge of the Truth, a Blessed Buddha, and he sees as it were face to face this Universe, freed from his senses in that they no longer can shape illusions to blind and deceive him, for with ordinary men their thought creates shapes about them, a false world in which they believe and are blinded. But it is not so with the Buddhas for they see things as they are. Then do they proclaim this truth of the Universe as it is, lovely in origin, lovely in progress, lovely in consummation, and this is to be known by the higher life, which is the Way to Wisdom in all its purity and perfectness."

And the Brahman Vasettha as in a dream, fixed, unconscious of all else, said:

"Speak, Lord,—I hear."

And the Lord said:

"There are two levels of the Way. One for the monk, one for the householder, and of the monk I speak first.

He takes nothing that is not his own. He is content with what is given, and honesty and a purè heart are his.

His life is pure, having put aside the habit and thought of sexual intercourse. This is for the householder only, but in all purity.

From truth in speech he cannot swerve, faithful and trustworthy, he hurts no man by deceit.

Slander is not for him, and calumny dies upon his tongue. He is a binder together of those who are divided, a peacemaker, a peace-lover, impassioned for peace.

From him come no harsh words. Whatever word is humane and lovely, pleasing and comforting, that he speaks.

Foolish talk and idle words are not his. In season he speaks what redounds to profit and wisdom.

He will not injure any creature. He eats but once a day. Gay and trivial shows are not for him. He does not adorn himself richly, for this is folly for a grown man.

For riches, be it in silver and gold and jewels, or flocks and herds he has no desire, and putting field to field does not tempt him who knows the world as it Is. And as for any deed of fraud or violence the possibility of it is not in him.

Nor will he teach magical spells nor gain a living or influence by any such arts or lying practices. And among the disturbed and careful, he moves serene and pure, as the moon, freed from clouds, pursues her way in midnight skies, shedding her light abroad to guide the wayfarer "

And Vasettha, musing, said:

" This is no low teaching. This is the way of a great nobleman, and such are his manners."

And the Blessed One:

" It is true. And there is more. Having attained right conduct within and without, he sets his mind free like a bird uncaged from the self, to pervade the four quarters of the world with love and sympathy, and as a mighty trumpeter makes himself heard with ease in all the four directions, so there is no living thing he passes by, but surrounds them with love grown great and beyond measure.

And when Love is attained, the way to be one with the Supreme is known and is not far from him."

And there was a silence, and the Brahman Vasettha said slowly:

" Venerable Gotama, I have been a liberal giver:

justly I sought riches, bountifully I bestowed them. Was this well ? "

And the Blessed One replied :

" Well. Yet have I shown you a more excellent way, for love is the path of wisdom to true understanding and union with all that is."

And the Brahman said with passion :

" Instruct me."

So the Perfect One opened to him the Way and, seated beside him, the Brahman Vasettha learned the Four Noble Truths of suffering, the truth, the cause, the cessation, and the way that leads to its extinction. And immediately there arose within him forgetfulness of all his riches and wisdom came upon him—the Light-bearer, so that he knew illusions for what they are and saw the Universe about him wholly fair, being united with it as a bridegroom with a bride. And seeing being substituted for blindness, he said :

" Most excellent, Lord, are the words of your mouth most excellent ! Just as if a man were to bring a lamp into the darkness so that all is seen clear, so is the truth made known by the Blessed One. And I, even I, betake myself to the Blessed One as my refuge, and to the Truth and the Brotherhood. May I be accepted ! "

And the Blessed One replied :

" Come, monk ! Well taught is the Doctrine. You have broken every fetter. You have made an end of pain."

So Vasettha was made one of the Brotherhood and glad at heart he exalted the word of the Blessed One.

And so it was that even the Shining Ones desired instruction of the Perfect One.

Thus have I heard.

When He who has thus Attained dwelt in the monastery of Jetavana, once there came to him a Shining One in the dead of night, and the place was lit up by the clear luminance that streamed from his body. And this Shining One placed himself neither too far nor too near, but where he should rightly be, and bowing low thus he addressed the Buddha:

"Most Excellent, during the twelve years of teaching many Shining Ones desiring to reach the holiness of the Peace have striven to discover what things are blessed, and still are ignorant. Instruct us therefore in those matters which are most blessed. Pronounce the Beatitudes."

And the Perfected One replied:

"Son of Light, to shun the company of the foolish, to pay homage to the learned, to worship what is worship-worthy, these are blessed things. Son of Light, mark them well.

"Son of Light, to dwell among good men: to hold within the consciousness of good deeds done in a former state of existence, to guard well the actions;—Son of Light, these are blessed things. Mark them well.

Son of Light, to hear and see much in order to acquire knowledge, to study all science that does not lead to sin, to use right language, to study right manners, these are blessed things. Son of Light, mark them well.

Son of light, to treat parents with tenderness and love, to guard wife and children, to do no evil when tempted, these are blessed things. Son of Light, mark them well.

Son of Light, to make offerings and give nobly, to follow the precepts of law and virtue, to assist relations and friends: these are blessed things, Son of Light, mark them well.

Son of Light, to avoid sin steadfastly, to abstain from strong drink, to lay up great treasure of good deeds: these are blessed things. Son of Light: mark them well.

Son of Light, to reverence those who are worthy of

veneration, to walk in humility, to dwell in content and gratitude, to hear the teaching of the Law; these are blessed things. Son of Light, mark them well.

Son of Light, be patient and endure suffering, to rejoice in good words, to visit saintly persons when possible, to talk on high matters; these are blessed things; Son of Light, mark them well.

"Son of Light, to practise holy austerities, to walk steadfast in the Truth with eyes fixed on the attainment of the Peace: these are blessed things. Son of Light, mark them well.

"Son of Light, to be unmoved, to be of serene mind, exempt from passion, composed and fearless amid all earthly dangers: these are blessed things. Son of Light, mark them well.

O Son of Light, whoever possesses these blessings shall never be overcome; shall in all things find joy. Son of Light, mark them well, thus attaining the peace of the Arhats, the Perfected Saints."

Thus replied the World-Honoured and the Shining One heard and went away content. And it is told that it was the beloved Ananda who handed down this discourse to the ages, having received it from the Blessed One, and mark it well, for in a little compass it contains all.

Praise be to the Possessor of the Six Glories, the Holy, the All-Wise!

Now of the bodily presence of the Blessed One will I say this.

When age came upon him it came with beauty, so that all hearts fell at his feet and embraced them because he was as one to whom all evil things must fly for refuge that being delivered from the self they might be made one with him and the Truth. And none could see him without this desire. Nor in his presence was virtue remembered for he was virtue's self made manifest in love, and in the ocean of love were all submerged who saw him.

His face was worn and calm as in an image of royal ivory, his nose prominent and delicate, bespeaking his Aryan birth, his eyes of a blue darkness, and he carried himself as one of the princes. But all this might be said of another, and there was none like him—none! For Wisdom walked on his left hand and Love on his right, and light as of the sun surrounded him. Wise and piercing were his words, delighting even those who would have scoffed.

And once the Holy One approached with his begging bowl the ploughed fields of a rich man and stood apart, waiting, and the man saw this, saying:

"Having ploughed and sown I eat. You also should plough and sow, for the idle shall not eat."

"I also, Brahman, plough and sow." Thus said the Perfected One.

"Yet we do not see the plough of the Venerable Gotama!" so said the other, mocking. And the World-Honoured answered:

"Faith is the seed, understanding the yoke and plough, tenderness the deliverance. So is my ploughing done. And the fruit is immortality, and having thus ploughed a man is freed of all ill."

And the Brahman poured rice-milk into a bowl and offered it, saying:

"Let the Blessed One eat of the rice-milk for he also is a ploughman who makes to grow the fruit of immortality."

And this man entered the Way and became glad at heart, having heard the Truth.

And the Holy One talked with men and women of all ranks and affairs, so that the mind of none was hidden from him, and, even as they felt, he knew, and their hopes and fears were not far from him. Fathomless were the wisdom and compassion of Him who has thus Attained.

So also with women, from the queens to the weaver-maidens they feared not to implore his mercy. Very patiently and according to the measure of their weakness he instructed them, and they grew like bamboos in a night shooting up to the light with glory of leaf and stem. And surely in these tender ones the Lord beheld the likeness of his mother, of whom it was said, "Joyful and reverenced of all, even as the young moon, strong and calm of purpose as the earth, pure of heart as the lotus, was Maya the Great Lady." And of these women many became nuns and teachers, and not a few attained unto the Perfect Enlightenment, passing even in this life into that Nirvana wherein are no more birth and death. And even the light women sought him in hope and he drove them not away, and wisdom rose within them like a wind of fire and burnt away all dross and alloy and they too entered the Way and wielded the powers, perceiving the Love in which all loves are one.

Yet let it not be thought that because of this compassion the Lord at any moment relaxed the watchfulness of those who followed him, knowing well that of all snares women may be the very worst. Stern were the rules he made for the men who live on the austere heights of contemplation, strait the fences about the way. For the householders, purity in marriage, kindness, reverence to mother, sister, wife, daughter, in their daily duties. For all, watchfulness and discipline lest the foot slip in the mire.

And one day, when they rested in the shade on a journeying, Ananda the well-beloved, cousin of the Lord, asked an instruction.

"Lord, how should we who are monks conduct ourselves with regard to women-kind, for this is a hard matter."

And the Excelling One said:

"See them not, Ananda."

"Even so, Lord. But if we should see them, what then?"

"Abstain from speech, Ananda."

"Even so, Lord. But if they should speak to us, what then?"

"Keep wide awake, Ananda."

And O that it were possible to set down the laughter of the Lord among his own, and the sweet converse when he related to them the stories of his former births, and whether parables or truths, how is it possible for the not wholly enlightened, who know not their own chains of births, to say? But wise were these stories and sweet and full of teaching for the little ones of the Law and babes might run to hear and laugh, and yet again the wisest pause and ponder the noble truths hidden in them.

Hear now a Birth Story of the Lord. For this is called the Holy Quail, and the Blessed One told it as he and his went through a jungle. For there a very great jungle fire arose and roared toward them very terribly, and some would have made counter-fire and burned the ground before it, but others cried aloud:

"Monks, what is it you would do? Surely it is madness, for we journey with the Master who can do All. And yet, making a counter-fire you would forget the power of the Buddhas! Come, let us go to the Master."

So they went, and the flame came roaring on to the place where they stood, and when it came within fifteen rods of the Blessed One it was extinguished like a torch plunged in water, and they magnified him. But he said:

"Monks, this was not due to my power but to the faith of a Quail. Hear this."

And they said:

"Even so, Lord."

And the beloved Ananda folded a robe and spread it as a seat and he sat and told this tale:

" In this very spot long, long ago, was a young Quail, and he lay in the nest and his parents fed him, for he could neither fly nor walk. And with a mighty roar there came a jungle fire and all the birds fled shrieking away and even his parents deserted him.

So the young Quail lay there alone, and he thought this:

" Could I fly, could I walk, I might be saved, but I cannot. No help have I from others and in myself is none. What then shall I do? "

And he reflected thus.

" In this world is Truth if it can be found. There are also the Buddhas who have seen the Truth and have shown it abroad, and in the Buddhas is love for all that lives. In me also is the Truth (though but a poor little Quail) and faith that has power. Therefore it behoves me, relying on these things, to make an Act of Faith and thus to drive back the fire and find safety for myself and the other birds."

So the Quail called to mind the Powers of the Buddhas, the Truth-Seers, and making a solemn asseveration of faith existing in himself he said this:

" Wings have I that cannot fly,  
Feet I have that cannot walk.  
My parents have forsaken me,  
O all-devouring fire, go back! "

And before this Act of Faith the fire dropped and died, retreating. And the Quail lived his life in the forest and passed away according to his deeds, and because of his strength of faith fire dies for ever when it touches this spot."

So said the Excellent One, and when he had finished

this discourse he made the connection and summed up, saying:

"My parents at that time were my present parents, and the Quail was I myself."

And they marvelled and were instructed.

And one day two monks approached him, having travelled far, and according to his manner he said in welcoming them:

"Is it well with you, monks? Are you able to live? Have you passed the rains in peace and unity, and have you experienced any lack of support?"

And they replied:

"It is not well with us, Blessed One, for there is great anger between us, and we devour our hearts with bitterness and know no peace."

And they laid their case before him in mutual hatred, and he said:

"He abused me! He beat me! In those who harbour such thoughts how can hatred die? By oneself evil is done. By oneself one suffers. The swans go on the path of sun, they go through the air by means of their miraculous power. In a man's power is his salvation from evil. There is no fire like passion: there is no losing throw like hatred. Let a man leave anger, let him forsake pride. Let him overcome anger by love and conquer the liar by truth. For hatred ceases not at any time by hatred, but only by love. This is an old rule."

An old rule. Yet when the Lord spoke it from his heart of bliss it became a new commandment and wisdom. So these two saluted one another in love before the face of the Perfect One, and, hand clasped in hand, they left him.

And again when a young monk was led away by the transient smile of a woman to his undoing, the Perfected One said this:

"Rise above the five senses which see things as they are not, and open the sight which see things as they are. Even the Divine Beings may well envy him whose desires like horses well broken are utterly subdued. Him whom no false desires can lead captive any more, by what temptation can he be felled—he the Awakened, the all-seeing, the desireless ? And make thought pure, for all that we are is the result of what we have thought. It is founded on our thoughts, it is made up of our thoughts. If a man speaks or acts from an evil thought pain follows him as the wheel follows the ox that draws the carriage. Earnest among the thoughtless, awake among the drowsy, the wise man presses steadily onward to joy."

And they said, "Even so, Lord." And seeing their faces glad about him, he added :

"As on a heap of refuse cast forth by the highway a lily may grow filling the air with sweetness, thus the disciples of the true Buddha shine forth among the people who walk in darkness."

And on another day when they talked of the lures of desire, the Lord said this :

"As long as the evil deed does not bear fruit the fool thinks it sweet as honey, but later comes the bitterness.

And when the evil deed is thrown upward in recklessness, like a stone it falls back on the fool and breaks his head.

For those who will not learn, who cannot as yet understand, hard to follow is the path of the wise man, like that of birds flying home through trackless depths of air. But what is difficult may with taking thought be done. The arrow-maker trues his arrow, the carpenter shapes his log, the wise man shapes himself, for no other hand can do it. Tranquil are his thoughts, serene his meditation when he has obtained freedom by knowledge. But the beginning is this—Let no man think lightly of the beginning of evil, saying—"It is only a little thing," for by the falling of water drops one by one, a pit is filled, and so is it with a little evil,—and with good it is the same. Little by little do good thoughts and deeds grow into the Peace.

By a man's self is evil done, by himself he suffers, by himself comes good, by himself purification, and by none other.

This is the sole victory that brings gladness, for in the world of forms victory breeds hatred for the conquered is unhappy. He who has given up both victory and defeat, he is the taster of bliss."

I write and men read, but who can declare the wisdom of the Lord? For as mists ascend at dawn so illusion was dispersed before his radiance and the veil was lifted and men beheld about them the true Universe of the Powers and the Truth,—the One, the Alone, in which we live and move and have our being. And it is within and without this world interpenetrating it, and those who know it possess the powers and walk like gods among men.

## CHAPTER XVIII

THUS have I heard:

Yet another thing, and heed it well for it was a day precious as clean gold.

As the Lord went with his disciples, they came to the river by the fields of Dhaniya the herdsman, a rich man who trusted in his goods, but kindly and simple, such as the Blessed One loved. And here he stayed his feet, smiling a little as at a thought of his own; and his disciples stood about him, and he said this:

"Here we see great riches of beasts and pasture; surely the man owning these good things is well content!"

And Dhaniya seeing the Holy One, drew near in his peasant's pride and addressed him:

"I have boiled my rice, I have milked my cows," so said the herdsman Dhaniya. "I dwell near the banks of the Mahi, my house is roofed, my fire kindled. Therefore, if thou wilt, rain, O sky!"

For believing his riches a strong shield he feared nothing.

"I am free from anger, free from stubbornness," said the Blessed One, "For one night I abide by the Mahi river. My house is unroofed, the fire of passion is extinguished. Therefore, if thou wilt, rain, O sky!" And he smiled.

"Gadflies are not found with me," said the herdsman Dhaniya. "In meadows rich with grass my cows are roaming, and well can they endure rain when it falls. Therefore if thou wilt, rain, O sky!"

"I have made a raft, I have passed over to the shore of the Peace," so said the Blessed One. "Therefore if thou wilt, rain, O sky!"

"My wife is obedient!" boasted the herdsman Dhaniya. "Winning she is, and I hear no ill of her. Therefore, if thou wilt, rain, O sky!"

"My mind is obedient, delivered from all worldly matters," so said the Blessed One. "And in me there is no ill. Therefore if thou wilt, rain, O sky!"

"I support myself by my own riches!" so said the herdsman Dhaniya, "and my children are healthy about me. I hear nothing wicked of them. Therefore if thou wilt, rain, O sky!"

"I am no one's servant," so said the Perfect One, "with what I have gained I wander through the world. For me there is no need to serve. Therefore, if thou wilt, rain, O sky!"

"I have cows, I have calves!" so said the herdsman Dhaniya. "I have also a bull as lord over the herds. Therefore if thou wilt, rain, O sky!"

"I have no cows, I have no calves!" so said the Happy One, "—And I have no bull as lord over the herds. Therefore, if thou wilt rain, O sky!"

"The stakes are driven in and cannot be shaken," so said the herdsman Dhaniya. "The ropes are new and well made: the cows cannot break them. Therefore if thou wilt, rain, O sky!"

"Having, like a bull, rent the ropes: having like an elephant broken through the tangle," so said the Blessed One, "I shall no more be born to death. Therefore if thou wilt, rain, O sky!"

And he smiled as one at rest, enthroned above pain or change.

Then all at once, from a full-wombed cloud, a shower poured down, filling both land and water. And the eyes of Dhaniya were enlightened, and seeing the true riches of the empty hand and freed soul, the herdsman spoke thus, bowing at the feet of the Perfect One.

"No small gain has indeed accrued to us since we have seen the Blessed One. We take refuge in thee, O Wisest. Be thou our Master."

"He who has cows has care with his cows," so said the Blessed One, concluding the matter. "But he who is free of these things has not care." So Dhaniya entered the Way of Peace, and taking the vow of the householder was at rest.

And now in this of Dhaniya is a thing much to be pondered. For it is observable that the Holy One said these words to him:

"I have passed over to Nirvana—to the Peace." How could this be and he yet living in the world of form? What then is the Nirvana? For, since the departing of Him who has thus Attained, the ignorant have taught the heresy which Sariputta the Great rebuked in the monk Yamaka—even that the true Nirvana is extinction, is dispersal of all that once was the man, the ego known to himself and others, he being annihilated in death as a flame blown out in vast darkness. Yet no, and again, not so, though not in words may the Truth be fully told. Yet—if a man may attempt to throw a stone at a star, this that follows may be told of the Nirvana.

They who talk of existence and non-existence are ignorant, for these are words only. There is no existence or non-existence, but in their stead reality and unreality, and in this world of form is unreality and in That World, reality. So that the unreal ego which we here believe to be the man is nothing and whether here or there has no reality but is a compound of causes which dissolve at death, while the reality of the man abides whether here or There. True it is that after death no longer can it be perceived, no longer can it be guessed by the bodily senses—the liars, the deceived, the slaves; yet in a profundity beyond all depths of all oceans it abides. The rest is silence.

Thus, the Blessed One and they who with him attained, were in life delivered from the illusion of the world of forms and seeing all as it is were glad. For the true Nirvana is an extinction—not of the eternal—but of craving, the lust of the flesh, the lust of life, and the pride of life. And when the inward fires of lust, and hatred and pride are extinguished, then that man has entered into the Nirvana whether here or there. And surely this was the Lesson of Lessons, and many a parable, many a teaching did the World-Honoured utter in all solemnity that we might know it is the self—the individual self lurking in a man like an ape in the boughs, clutching, greedy, foul, foolish, that is the cause of all evil and sorrow and of his separation from the universe of life and light that lies about him. And he must learn that this foul and foolish chatterer is dream and illusion of the senses and consciousness, For when this teaching is mastered we lift the true eyes of wisdom and look about us seeing at last that the world is wholly fair. Know this, for it is the very kernel of the nut. This is the Way of Peace, this is the Gate of the Ten Perfections whereby we also are perfect being One; this is the Nirvana, absolute in joy and bliss immortal.

Be not misled. If this false belief of annihilation be accepted the belief in the Karma and its awful justice falls to the ground, and the Blessed One is made to utter words unreal and deceptive. It is not well to traduce the teaching of the Blessed One, for what he taught he knew, and where he was silent it was from knowledge too great to be uttered save to his high initiates, and they too, knowing, were content. For a man can but receive as he is able, and the Truth needs two servants—the one to speak and the other to hear.

True is it that the Lord before he passed away from the world of the senses said to the beloved Ananda, this:

"I have preached the truth, Ananda, and in respect of the Truth He who has thus Attained had no such thing as the closed fist of the Teacher who holds back his knowledge."

Yes, but a man can but take what he can, and where the great saints of the Lord knew and were content, the lesser men guessed and stumbled blindly by excess of light and this was unavoidable for they were not prepared, and in future lives they have learned, will learn, and they too be content in wisdom.

Therefore when men ask the disciple of the Nirvana, and say:

"Is it annihilation? Is it the end of all, for so many teach?" reply thus:

"It is the annihilation of ignorance and passion and all their brood. It is the annihilation of conditioned being and of all the illusion that fettered us. It is the rending of the painted veil of life that hides from us the light. It is the end of all turning of the wheel of the long pilgrimage through self-shaped dream-worlds of deception. It is the end of grief and self-deceit. It is awakening from the dream of life, from the crippling of the ego-self, into freedom. It is beyond all that we call life, and death is unknown to it. It is All and One and above right and wrong and in it are all things reconciled.

"And it is us and in us and we in it for ever."

Open the eyes of understanding and see and know, as he the Awakened, has taught.

And now must the story turn to the Princess Yashodara, released from grief and grown strong in wisdom.

Musing night and day on these thoughts and this blessedness the Princess excelled in knowledge and in her true eyes the light shone brighter and more bright in the deep contemplation of her heart, and when in the passing of the years the wealth of the Maharaja fell into her hands she valued it nothing, placing it where most good and least harm could flow from it. And with attendant princesses she walked nearly five hundred miles, refusing all offers of assistance, that she might be near the World-Honoured, breathing the same air, sometimes attendant upon his teaching, sometimes sending dutifully to inquire after the health of the monk Rahula, her son.

So, having grown old, but still eminent in the nobility of her beauty and its calm, as she sat alone one day she remembered many of her friends who through the Peace here to be attained had departed to that Other. And she thought this:

"I was born on the same day as my lord, the Awakened One, and in the regular order of things I should on the same day enter the Great Peace. But this is an honour too great for me and far beyond my deserts, nor can it be. I am now seventy-eight years in this world of illusion, and in two years from now, he, the Blessed One, will enter that which cannot be named. I will therefore request permission to precede him, as the lower should precede the great."

So, accompanied by her attendants, the Princess went to the Vihara, the monastery, where the Lord sat at the time with a company of disciples, and presenting herself before him humbly asked forgiveness for any faults she might have committed. And he replied:

"You are the most virtuous of women. But from the time you received the Light, you have done no marvels, so that many have not known the power that is in you, doubting whether you were indeed an Arhat. There is a company assembled about us, who know not the Powers. Show them."

But the Princess, doubting in her humility that this should be, doubting whether a woman should display the beauty of her person to onlookers, was not assured that this was well. Yet, with the insight to which time is nothing, she spoke, rehearsing the mystery and marvel of all her former lives, for now having vanquished rebirth she was as the traveller who nearing the mountain top and the eternal purities sees the way by which he has come, rejoicing in perils escaped and rest unending. And all sat entranced, listening to the music of her voice and the marvels she—to whom time was no more than a child's toy cast aside—unfolded before them. And suddenly, as she ended, the air upbore her light feet and a marvel was done before them, for in the air she prostrated herself before Him who has thus Attained, attributing to him the knowledge that had guided her into bliss. And those who saw hid their faces.

And when all was concluded she retired to her own dwelling and there, that same night, rising from contemplation to contemplation, she beheld the Peace, being delivered for ever from all illusion, and so passed into That which is to come.

And of her son—the monk Rahula—this also must be told:

At one time the Lord, with robe and bowl, went to Savatthi in search of alms, and his son Rahula followed step for step, and the Blessed One, turning, said this:

" Whatever form one bears, monk, is to be viewed with perfect wisdom and the understanding—' This is not mine; it is not I. This is not my true self.' "

And Rahula answered:

" And only form, O Lord, and only form, O Happy One?"

" Form, Rahula, and sensation and perception and the tendencies and consciousness. These also are not the true self."

And Rahula, being thus addressed with an Instruction, would not go to roam and beg among the people, but set aside his bowl, and sat beneath a tree to meditate upon the Instruction. And in the evening, having ended his calm contemplation, he sought the Blessed One and saluting him reverently seated himself respectfully beside him and besought him to instruct him on the discipline of meditation and training, and the Blessed One instructed him in all the processes, even to the ruling of the breath in inspiration and expiration so that the false senses may be lulled and the true eye of wisdom opened, and pleased and gladdened was the venerable Rahula with that high instruction.

And thus Rahula in time became first a great warrior for the Truth and then a great Arhat: a perfected saint. And in what way did he become a warrior? Even as a monk asked of the Awakened One:

" Warriors, warriors, we call ourselves, O Happy One, and in what way are we warriors?" and had this reply:

" We make war, monk. Therefore are we warriors?"

" And for what do we make war, O Leader?"

" For perfect virtue, for high endeavour, for sublime wisdom. To see in a world of blindness, to be free in a world of slaves,—therefore, do we make war."

And when is the victory gained?—When the dark night of I-ness is enlightened,—when the man is no longer a swimmer struggling for life in agony against the waves, but the gray gull borne on the winds in bliss or floating at peace on the billows of eternity.

This is the victory of the monk Rahula and of the wise.

# Part IV

## CHAPTER XIX

So continued our Lord, wandering from place to place, or resting in the season of the rains in the monasteries provided by the supporters of the Brotherhood, and, followed by his own, he taught the Breaking of the Fetters—and the fetters he broke are these:

The delusion of self—namely that the individual ego is real and self-existent. For what can exist outside the Universal Self? And egoism is the very root of death.

Doubt. For who can advance boldly, doubting the way and where he shall set the next step?

Belief in good works and ceremonies. For what good work can open a man's eyes if his motive is mean, and what value have rites and ceremonies in themselves?

Fleshly lust. By no means did the Lord command a cruel asceticism, for this he had tried to the uttermost and having laid it aside, passed on. No, but a joyous temperance, the child of wisdom and duty, the fosterer of endeavour. And duty in all things, a strength by some to be attained now, by others with patience in later lives.

Ill-will. For this is a cruel fetter, biting to the very bone of the wretch who carries it, and it is forged indeed from the black iron of egoism and belief in the separate ego.

And this being all accomplished the last fetters to be broken are:

The desire for separate and individual life in the world of forms we see about us.

The desire for separate life in the formless world to which we shall attain.

Pride—the very snarer of Divine Beings.

Self-righteousness, the womb-sister of pride.

And last, the most terrible of fetters—

Ignorance—mother of a deadly brood.

And where he went these fetters fell before him, and prison doors were opened and they who had sat in darkness walked in light. And they aspired to perfection for he taught that Perfection was their heritage, if not now, then in some future life where the sown seeds of good expanding should throw out strong arms and glorious blossom.

And they believed, and some set tottering steps in the path, and some advanced with wings rather than feet, but all were seekers and finders.

But he compelled none, nor threatened, for by a man's true self comes his salvation, and seated among his own he said:

"The Tathagata—He who has thus Attained, does not think that it is he who must lead the Brotherhood or that the Order is dependent upon him."

Only, steadfastly pointing the way, he rejoiced that men should follow it, casting forth his light like the sun, not compelling men to guide their steps by it.

Nor did he teach resignation to sorrow nor its acceptance as a blessing and discipline. Far from it. For in the clear percipience of the Lord sorrow is ignorance and shameful.

"One thing only, monks, now as always I declare to you—sorrow and the uprooting of sorrow."

For what man would wander in the mist of sorrow when he may walk glad and straight to the goal in the sunlight of wisdom. And sorrow understood is sorrow ended.

Therefore the Lord taught understanding of sorrow as the first need, and therefore says the wise Nagasena ;

" As a boy I was admitted to the Order, and nothing did I know of the goal. But I thought—' These men taught by the Awakened One will teach me.' And they taught, and now I know with understanding the foundation and the crown of Renunciation."

And what the Lord taught he knew : that there is no sorrow for the wise.

And thus when he stayed at Alavi, by the cattle-path in the forest he rested on a couch of leaves, and it so chanced that a man of Alavi as he went through the forest saw the Exalted One sitting absorbed in meditation, and greeting him with respect this man sat down at his side and said :

" Master, does the World-Honoured live happily ? "

And the Perfect One answered :

" It is so, young man. Of those who live happily in the world I also am one."

" Cold, Master, is the winter night, the time of frost is coming : rough is the ground trodden by cattle : thin is the couch of leaves : light the monk's yellow robe : sharp the cutting winter wind."

For his heart pitied the ageing of the Exalted One. But he replied, again smiling :

" It is so, young man. I live happily. Of those who live happily in the world I also am one."

And so it was, and with his own also. For his mendicants rejoicing said to one another :

" We who call nothing our own, drenched with happiness, we in this world cast out light like the radiant Gods."

And their song was—

"Abolished is the round of birth: Completed the ascetic life;
Done what was to do.
This world of form is no more. This we know."

And sometimes proud and learned Brahmans would come to dispute haughtily with the Perfect One, and they, full of pride and anger, would rage and trip in their discourse thinking to show their much learning rather than to seek the truth. But like the waves of a muddy river lashing rock so were they, and the Lord sat there always, answering duly, teaching duly, clothed in serenity, his skin the colour of bright gold, his eyes bright and calm, for he said:

"That in disputation with anyone whatsoever I could be thrown into any confusion or embarrassment,—there is no possibility of such a thing, and because I know of no such possibility I remain quiet and confident. And even when I am carried here upon a bed shall my intellectual strength remain unabated."

And his monks said:

"Truly from the Exalted One comes all our wisdom."

And because he was so near the Blessed One many monks would come to the venerable Ananda and say:

"It is long, brother, since we heard a discourse from the Exalted One. It were very good if we might hear one now."

"Well, venerable ones, betake yourselves to the hermitage of the Brahman Rammako. Perhaps you will get to hear a discourse from the lips of the Exalted One." For Ananda was wise in the ways of the Master.

Now after the Perfected One had returned from his begging-round, he turned and said:

"Come, Ananda, let us go to the East Grove, to the terrace of the Mother of Migara, and stay there until the evening."

So they went, and when he had finished his meditation he turned to the venerable Ananda:

" Come, Ananda, let us go to the Old Bath and refresh our limbs."

So they went. Then the beloved Ananda addressed the Perfected One thus:

" The hermitage of the Brahman Rammako, Master, is not far from here. It is pleasantly situated in peaceful solitude. Good were it if the Master should betake himself there."

And the Blessed One signified by silence his assent. And there they found many monks in edifying discourse. And he waited till they were done, and cleared his throat and rapped at the knocker, and they opened the door, and the World-Honoured entered in and seated himself and incited and gladdened them all with great and high discourse.

So they got what they needed, for very wise was the beloved Ananda in dealing with the Master.

Amazing indeed were the experiences of those who followed the Lord, and not to be understood of those who have not stood face to face with Truth and Love unveiled and terrible in beauty, and terrible also in the loves they inspire. What can words avail?

And where he went the Awakened One strewed little precepts like flowers, easy for a child to remember yet each an upward spiral on the Way.

" If all knew the fruits of almsgiving as I, monks, know them, most surely they would not eat the last least mouthful without dividing it with another."

And they answered, " Even so, Lord," and gave of their food, living in peace amidst the Transient, until even its semblance should pass for ever away. And nothing else than food had they to give, being monks.

And one asked of the learned nun Dhammadhina;

" And how, venerable Lady,—how and what has the

Blessed One taught about the arising of the false ego in the beginning of things? How came it to be? What does he teach of this?"

"It is the lust of life that sows repeated being in successive lives."

"And how is the annihilation of the false ego to be attained, Venerable Lady? How has the Exalted One taught?"

"Even by the complete annihilation, rejection, and driving forth of the lust of life—this is what was taught by the Exalted One." So answered the nun Dhammadhina. "Even through the breaking of any attachment to the Transient."

But of how Attachment began to be in the beginning of things the Lord would not answer. The Way out, he taught; the way in concerns not at all the man who is fleeing for his life to peace and safety from attachment to the Transient and its illusion.

And again,—

"But what follows after death? What follows after the extinction of illusion?" the seeker asked of the learned nun Dhammadhina. And she replied:

"Abandon the question, brother. I cannot grasp the meaning of the question. If you will, go to the Enlightened One and ask him."

And he went, and the Lord answered:

"Wise is Dhammadhina and mighty in understanding. My answer is hers."

For the Unknown cannot be known until the way is built to it. Build then the way, and knowledge will come in time. But, without words, to the few, the very few, this knowledge has come, as has been told.

And when the nun Gotami asked him:

"Will the Exalted One teach me the very quintessence of the Law," he answered thus:

"Whatever teaching leads to passion and not to peace

to pride and not to humility, to desire of much in place of little, to love of society and not of solitude, to idleness and not to striving, to a mind of unrest and not to a mind at peace—that, O Gotami,—note well!—that is not the way,—that is not the teaching of the Master."

And as they sat in the calm of the sunset and discoursed, Sariputta the Great said this:

"I desire not life. I desire not death. I wait until my hour shall come like a servant that waits for his wage. I await the coming of the hour, conscious and of thoughtful mind."

Thus steadfast in the way they continued, not cruelly mortifying the body but in the true asceticism of the heart that cannot be tempted. For the Awakened One said this:

"I teach asceticism inasmuch as I teach the burning away of all evil conditions of the heart. And the true ascetic who thus lives may fitly and rightly eat of the food that is given him in alms, of rice pleasantly prepared and such-like, and it will do him no ill."

So quietly and in radiance life went on as a summer day which from dewy dawn passes through every gradation of light until the night comes, taking the world in her net of stars and laying all to rest.

And still the Exalted One journeyed and taught, now being very aged, and the seeds of his doctrine were carried as if by far-flying birds into the outer lands which had never felt in this life the tread of his blessed feet nor seen the calm of his face nor the majesty that attended him. And taking root these seeds shot up later into mighty trees of glorious growth.

And still he journeyed to and fro, and the people said to the monks:

"Let not the World-Honoured overweary himself, for in what are we worthy that our well-being should cost the world its Light?"

And they answered :

" All he does is well. This also is well and could not be otherwise."

But the beloved Ananda saw with fear that the World-Honoured moved more slowly and with more painful effort on each journey he made. And awe and grief possessed Ananda, seeing this, for he had not as yet attained to perfect enlightenment,—and with many cares he compassed the Blessed One and followed him wherever he went.

# CHAPTER XX

## THE LAST JOURNEY

AND the Blessed One passed through Pataligama and went on to the river, and at that time Ganges was swollen and brimming, and some with him began to seek for boats and some for basket-rafts that they might pass over. But the Exalted One, swiftly as a powerful man could stretch out his arm and withdraw it, vanished from the hither side of the river and stood on the other bank with the brethren. And he uttered this verse:

"Those who cross the stormy sea
Making a firm way for their feet,
While the blinded tie their basket-rafts,
These are the wise, these are the safe and glad."

And they passed on to the village of Nadika, and at the last the Happy One rested at the Brick Hall, and the beloved Ananda (who tended him always) came and sat down respectfully beside him, and having passed through the village and heard of the deaths of several devout followers, men and women, who had followed them formerly, he asked the Lord of their destiny and of what had befallen them.

And naming them each and all by name, replied the Exalted One:

"Of those men and women there are some who in their first return to this world will make an end of sorrow and illusion and return no more. And some there are for whom having attained the highest knowledge, it is no longer possible that they should return to mortal birth, for they are now assured of final salvation."

And in the Brick Hall at Nadika he taught the people, saying:

"Great is the fruit, great the advantage of earnest contemplation when adorned with right doing. And great the fruit of high intellect adorned with earnest contemplation. For the mind set round with intelligence is thus delivered from sensuality, from the false ego, from delusion and ignorance."

And they went on to Vaisali, and from thence to Beluva, and there the Blessed One rested in the village. And he said to the brethren:

"Mendicants, do you take up your abode round about Vaisali for the rains, each according to his friends. For I shall enter upon the rainy season here at Beluva."

"So be it, Lord," said the brethren in assent, and so it was done.

Now when the Blessed One had thus entered on the rains at Beluva there fell upon him a sickness, and sharp pains came upon him even to death. But mindful and self-possessed he bore them without complaint. And this thought came into his mind:

"It would not be right for me to pass away without addressing the disciples, without taking leave of the Order. Let me now by a strong effort of the will bend down this sickness and keep my hold on life until the allotted time be come."

And he bent that sickness down and it abated.

And when he began to recover he went out of the little vihara—the monastery, and sat down behind it on a seat spread out for him. And the venerable Ananda went where the Blessed One was, and sat respectfully beside him, and said this:

"I have seen, Lord, how the Blessed One suffered, and though at that sight my body became weak as a creeper, yet I had some little comfort in thinking that the Blessed One would not pass from existence until at least he had left some instructions touching the Order."

"What then, Ananda? Does the Order expect that of me? Now, He who has thus Attained thinks not that it is he who shall lead the Order or that it is dependent upon him. I too, Ananda, am now grown old and full of years. My journey is drawing to its close. I have reached my sum of days, I am turning eighty years of age. And just as a worn-out cart can only with much additional care be made to move, so, I think, the body of the Tathagata can only be kept going with much additional care. It is only when ceasing to attend to any outward thing he becomes plunged in devout meditation concerned with no material object,—it is only then that the body of the Tathagata is at ease."

And there was a long pause, and the venerable Ananda remained steadfastly gazing at the Perfect One, absorbed in his words as foreseeing the end. And the Lord resumed:

"Therefore, Ananda, be lamps unto yourselves. Betake yourselves to no external Refuge. Hold fast to the truth as a lamp. Look not for refuge to any one beside yourselves. And whoever after I am dead shall be a lamp unto themselves and holding fast to the truth look for refuge to no one outside themselves, it is they, among my mendicants, who shall reach the Height."

And again the Blessed One robed himself early in the morning and taking his bowl went into Vaisali for alms, and when he returned he sat down upon the seat prepared for him and when he had finished eating the rice he said:

"Take up the mat, Ananda,—I will go to spend the day at the Kapila Ketiya."

"So be it, Lord," said the venerable Ananda, and he followed step for step behind the Blessed One.

And when he had come there the Blessed One sat down upon the mat spread out for him, and the venerable Ananda took his seat respectfully beside him. And the Blessed One said:

"Whoever, Ananda, has developed himself and ascended to the very heights of the four paths to Power, thus transcending bodily conditions and using these Powers for good may, if he desires it, remain in the same birth for an age, or that portion of the age which is yet to run. Now He who has thus Attained has developed these Powers and could therefore live on yet for an age or that portion of the age which has yet to run."

But even though this suggestion was given by the Blessed One, the venerable Ananda did not comprehend it, nor did he say, "Vouchsafe, Lord, to remain! Live on for the good and happiness of the peoples, out of pity for the world and the weal of Divine Beings and men."

And a second time did the Blessed One say this, and yet did not the beloved Ananda speak.

Now the Blessed One addressed him thus:

"You may leave me, Ananda, for awhile."

And rising from his seat, Ananda saluted the Lord, and sat down at the foot of a tree not far off, and when he was gone, the Evil One, the Tempter, approached the Lord and stood beside him, and he said:

"Pass away now, Lord, from existence. Let the Blessed One die. For did he not say that when the Order was established, and the lay-people, and the truth made known, that then the time would be come? And all this is now done, and the time is here. Pass away now, therefore, Lord. Let the Blessed One die."

And when he had spoken, the Blessed One said to the Evil One:

" Be happy. At the end of three months from this time the Blessed One will die."

Thus did the Lord deliberately and consciously reject the rest of his possible sum of life. And there followed an earthquake and tremblings and thunders.

And Ananda returned in haste and said:

" Wonderful and marvellous is this earthquake, Lord, and what is its cause ? "

And the Lord said:

" Of the eight causes of earthquake and tremblings, this is one—when an Awakened One,—He who has thus Attained, consciously and deliberately rejects the remainder of his life, then is the earth shaken."

And, still speaking of the mastery of the Powers, the Lord continued:

" Now I call to mind, Ananda, how when I used to enter into an assembly of many hundred nobles with discourse of religion I would instruct and gladden them, and they would say,—' Who may this be who thus speaks ? A man or a God ? ' And having taught and gladdened them, suddenly I would vanish away. But they knew me not even when I vanished away, and they would say in bewilderment, ' Who may this be who has thus vanished away ? A man, or a God ? "

And he spoke also of the eight stages of deliverance from errors of perception, passing beyond the apprehension of form through infinite space and infinite reason and finally beyond sensation and ideas, even into the eighth stage of deliverance.

And having given this instruction the Lord related to the venerable Ananda how that in three months' time he should hear his voice no more, and the venerable Ananda cried out vehemently:

" Vouchsafe, O Blessed One, to live. Stay with us for the weal of Divine Beings and men."

But the Lord answered:

"The time for making such a request is past."

And a second and a third time Ananda entreated and the Lord replied, saying:

"Verily, the word has gone forth from Him who has thus Attained. That the Tathagata for the sake of living should repent of that saying can in no wise be. Come, Ananda, let us rise and go to the Mahavana."

And they went to the Mahavana, to the Service Hall, and he commanded Ananda to assemble there such of the brethren as dwelt in the neighbourhood of Vaisali. And when they were assembled the Blessed One sat down upon his mat and addressed them. And he said:

"The truths, monks, which I have made known to you and you have mastered, these practise, meditate, and spread abroad, that it may continue to be for the good and happiness of great multitudes.

"Behold, monks, now I exhort you. All component things must grow old and pass away. Work out your salvation with diligence. At the end of three months from this time He who has thus Attained will die. My age is now full ripe: my life draws to its close. I leave you, I depart, relying on myself alone. Be earnest, holy, full of thought. Be steadfast in resolve. Keep watch over your own hearts. Who wearies not, but holds fast to the Law, shall cross this sea of life, shall make an end of grief."

So he spoke, and they dispersed silently.

And the Blessed One robed himself early in the morning and took his bowl and went into Vaisali for alms, and when he had eaten his meal and was returning, he gazed steadfastly at Vaisali and he said this:

"This is the last time, Ananda, that He who has thus Attained will behold Vaisali. Let us now go to Bhandagama."

And they went, and the Lord rested in the village

itself, and there he addressed the brethren, saying:

"It is through ignorance of the Truths that we have had to run so long, to wander so far in this weary road of rebirth—you and I. But when the noble conduct of life, noble meditation, noble wisdom and noble freedom are realised and known, then is the craving for existence rooted out, the chain broken and we return to earth no more."

And it was there also that he delivered the high discourse on the nature of the Four Truths; and having done this he pressed on with the venerable Ananda and a great company of his own to Pava. And there he stayed in the Mango Grove of Chunda, and Chunda was a smith by family.

And when Chunda heard that the Perfect One had come to Pava and rested in his Mango Grove, he went to him and saluted him joyfully, and with reverence took his seat beside him, and the Blessed One gladdened him with talk of high things. And, so gladdened, he addressed the Lord, and said:

"May the Blessed One do me the honour of taking his meal, together with the brethren, at my house tomorrow?"

And the Lord signified by silence his consent, and seeing he had consented, Chunda the worker in metals bowed before him and, keeping him on his right hand, departed.

And at the end of the night Chunda made ready in his house excellent food, hard and soft, sweet rice and cakes and the food, found in the earth and loved by boars, truffles, and when all was ready he announced it to the Lord, saying:

"Exalted One, the meal is ready."

And the Blessed One robed himself and took his bowl and he and his followers went to the dwelling-place of Chunda. And when the meal was over, he gladdened the smith with discourse of high matters, and so rose and departed.

But after the Blessed One had eaten of his food then fell upon him a grievous disease, and sharp pain came upon him even to death, but he bore it without complaint, mindful and self-possessed. And to the venerable Ananda he said:

"Come, let us go to Kusinara."

"Even so, Lord," said the venerable Ananda.

And they went, but as they went the Blessed One grew very weary and he rested beneath a tree and said:

"Fold the robe and spread it for me, I pray you. I am weary, Ananda, and I must rest awhile."

And the robe was spread, folded fourfold, and when the World-Honoured was seated he asked for fresh water to drink and Ananda answered:

"But, Lord, five hundred carts have just gone by across the stream and stirred up by the wheels it has become fouled and turbid. Let us wait for the river, cool and transparent, easy to get into. There the Blessed One may drink and cool his limbs."

But his thirst would not wait, and taking a bowl Ananda went down to the stream, and when he came to it it flowed clear as light. And he thought:

"How wonderful, how marvellous is the power of Him who has thus Attained. For this turbid stream is flowing brightly now."

And when he returned he said:

"Great is the power of the Lord. Let the Happy One drink!"

Now at that time a young man named Pukkusa, a disciple of the Brahman Alara, passed along the highway, and seeing the Blessed One very weary beneath the tree he came and saluted him taking his seat respectfully beside him, and the Holy One discoursed with him on the depths of calm in pure contemplation and abstraction of mind from the vain shows about us, and with every power of his mind and heart did the young man listen, and when the great teaching was ended, he said:

"Most excellent, Lord, are the words of your mouth—most excellent. As it were to bring a lamp into the darkness so are your words. And I, even I, betake myself to the Blessed One as my refuge to the Truth and the Brotherhood. May I be accepted as a disciple!"

And the young Pukkusa presented two robes of burnished cloth of gold to the World-Honoured, saying:

"May favour be shown and these accepted at my hand!"

"In that case, Pukkusa, offer the one to me and the other to Ananda."

And so it was done and the young man, gladdened and strengthened, rose and bowed down and went his way.

## CHAPTER XXI

Now not long after the young man was gone the venerable Ananda placed that glorious robe upon the Blessed One, and so placed it appeared to dim and lose its splendour, and Ananda said:

"Lord, it is marvellous that the colour of the skin of the Blessed One should now be so clear, so bright, beyond measure, for this robe of burnished gold has lost its splendour in the radiance."

"It is even so, Ananda. For on the night that He who has thus Attained achieves supreme Enlightenment, and also on the night in which he passes away for ever leaving no residue behind, the colour of his person becomes exceedingly bright and clear. And now this day at the third watch of the night at Kusinara, between the twin sala trees the utter passing away of Him who has thus Attained will take place. Come, let us go forward."

And when he was come to the Mango Grove by the river, he said:

"Fold a robe for me, Kundaka, for I am forespent and would lie down." And it was done and the Blessed One laid himself down on his right side, and meditated, calm and self-possessed, and finally, calling to Ananda the beloved, he said:

"Now it may happen that some one may grieve Chunda the smith, saying, 'It is evil to you, Chunda, and loss, that the Blessed One died after he had eaten his last meal from your provision.' But check this remorse,

Ananda, by saying—' It is good and gain to you, Chunda, that this should have been. For the very mouth of the Blessed One has told me this—There is laid up for Chunda the smith a good Karma of long life and good fortune and good fame and the inheritance of Heaven and sovereign power.' In this manner check any remorse in Chunda the smith."

Then once more rising, the World-Honoured began again his pilgrimage of pain, and he said:

" Come, let us go to the Sala Grove of the Malla people at Kusinara."

And they went on.

So with the monks the Exalted One reached at last the Sala Grove of the Mallas, and he desired that Ananda the beloved would lay a couch for him with its head to the north between the twin sala trees that they knew. And this was done, and the sala trees shed their dropping blossoms on the body of the Blessed One, for so it must be with a departing Buddha.

And here, Ananda seeing that the time drew on, reverently besought the commands of the Lord as to the disposal of his mortal body. And he replied:

" Hinder not yourselves by honouring what remains of Him who has thus Attained. Be zealous, I beseech you, in your own behalf: be intent on good. There are wise men among the nobles who will do due honour to the body of the Tathagata."

And when he heard this Ananda could no longer endure his grief, and that the Lord might not see his tears, he went into the monastery and stood leaning against the door and wept, for he thought:

" Alas! I still remain but a learner, one who has not yet attained perfection, and the Master is about to pass away from me—he who is so kind."

But the Blessed One called the brethren and asked:

" Where then, monks, is Ananda?"

And they told him, and he said to a certain brother:

"Go, brother, and say 'Brother Ananda, the Master calls you.'"

And it was done and the beloved Ananda returned, and the Blessed One said to him.

"Enough, Ananda. Do not let yourself be troubled. Do not weep. Have I not often told you that it is in the very nature of things most near and dear to us that we must divide ourselves from them and leave them? How then could it be possible that anything containing within itself the necessity of dissolution should not be dissolved? For a long time, Ananda, have you been very near to me by acts of love, kind and good, that never varies and is beyond all measure. And not only by acts but by words and thoughts of love. You have done well, Ananda. Be earnest in effort and you too shall soon be delivered and attain the perfect percipience."

Then the Blessed One said to the others:

"He is a wise man, monks, is Ananda. Knowing what is right he has four marvellous qualities, for those who see him, who hear him speak or teach are filled with joy on beholding and hearing him, and the company of the Assembly are ill at ease when Ananda is silent."

And later he said:

"Go now, Ananda, to the town of Kusinara and inform the people of the Mallas that in the last watch of the night He who has thus Attained will pass away. And say this—'Be favourable herein, Mallas, and leave no occasion to reproach yourselves that you did not visit the World-Honoured in his last hours.'"

And Ananda the beloved went, robed and carrying his bowl and attended by a member of the Order.

And, as it chanced, the Mallas were assembled in the Council Hall and when they heard his words, they wept, they and their wives and children, saying:

"Too soon will the Blessed One die!
Too soon will the Happy One pass away.
Too soon will the Light of the World be darkened!"

And trooping out with their wives and children, these Mallas came to the Grove of the sala trees, and Ananda considering their great number thought:

"There is not time that they should speak singly with the Lord. But I will present them by families."

And this he did, causing the Mallas to stand in groups and so presented them, saying:

"Lord, a Malla of such and such a name, with his wives, his children his retinue and his friends, humbly bows down at the feet of the Blessed One." And that family with its retinue then advanced, weeping.

And after this manner were all presented during the first watch of the night, and when it was done they retired in heavy grief.

But there was yet one work of mercy left unto the Lord. For at this time a mendicant named Subaddha was dwelling at Kusinara, and he heard the news that the Blessed One was about to pass away and his religious doubts rushed into his mind and he thought:

"Seldom indeed in this world do the authentic Buddhas appear. I have faith in the monk Gotama that he may be able to remove my uncertainty. I will go to him."

And he went and told his case to Ananda and he replied:

"Enough, friend Subaddha. Do not trouble Him who has thus Attained. The Lord is weary."

And three times he refused. But the Lord heard and he said:

"Let him come to me. He will ask from a true desire of knowledge and will quickly understand my replies."

So Ananda said:

" Enter in, friend Subaddha. The Blessed One gives you leave."

And speaking respectfully that mendicant put his questions, awaiting the answer with anxiety. And it was this : Is the Way of the Law the only path possible for a saint? Can that way alone produce sainthood of the first order? "

And the Lord replied :

" Perfect saints from the first to the fourth degree are found only in the Noble Eightfold Path."

And when he had given the reason why only under such discipline is perception perfected, Subaddha, hailing his words with gladness, every doubt lost in light, besought admission as a disciple and it was granted and the probation of four months remitted, though Subaddha himself willingly undertook that probation. But the Lord said :

" In this case I acknowledge the difference in persons."

And this was the last man the Lord himself received. And because it could not be otherwise Subaddha attained light and percipience, and became conscious that for him birth was at an end, and he became a great Arhat. And he sat beside the Blessed One until the end.

And now the time drew on swiftly and, knowing this, the Blessed One said, while they all stood in great grief surrounding him :

" It may be, Ananda, that in some of you the thought may arise—' Now that the word of the Master is ended we have no Teacher.' But this is not so. The truths and the rules of the Order—let them be your Teacher when I am gone. And when I am gone, Ananda, let the Order, if it will, abolish the Lesser Precepts."

And after awhile the Blessed One spoke again, and he said :

" It may be, brethren, that there is doubt or misgiving in the mind of some brother as to the Buddha, the

Truth, the Way. Inquire freely, monks! Do not reproach yourself afterwards with the thought,—'We were face to face with the Blessed One, and yet could not bring ourselves to inquire.'"

But the brethren were silent. And again and a third time the Lord repeated this. And in his care for them he said:

"It may be that the brethren will not question out of reverence for the Teacher. Let one friend then communicate with another."

And still they were silent, and the venerable Ananda said:

"It is wonderful, Lord. I have faith to believe that in this whole Assembly of the brethren there is not one who has any doubt or misgiving as to the Buddha, the Truth, or the Way."

And the Blessed One, sinking yet lower into weakness, answered:

"From the fullness of faith do you speak, Ananda. But He who has thus Attained knows of certain knowledge that in this whole Assembly there is not one brother who has any doubt or misgiving. For even the most backward of all these brethren knows and has seen and will be born no more in a state of suffering and is assured of final peace."

And by these words did the World-Honoured reassure Ananda the beloved in whom as yet the tenderness of love crippled its wings, restraining it from the eagle-flight of the perfected Arhat.

And Ananda knelt, hiding his face beside the sala trees where lay the Blessed One, for he knew that the parting drew very near. And there was a deep silence, and it was as though all the spirits of earth and air, and the Divine Beings and the Three Worlds, the earth, the heavens, and hells waited with them nor would lose a breath that remained. And He who has thus Attained lay with closed eyes, submerged in calm as in a great ocean.

And after awhile his eyelids opened and for the last time he looked upon them, and for the last time his disciples heard his voice, strong in death:

"Behold now, brethren, I exhort you, saying—'Decay is inherent in all component things. Work out your own salvation with diligence.'"

And they trembled, kneeling about him.

Then the Blessed One entered into the first state of ecstasy, and, rising from this, into the second, and so passed into the third and into the fourth, and rising from that realm of ecstasy he entered the realm of the infinity of space, and from this he entered the realm of the infinity of consciousness, and rising from this he entered the realm of nothingness, and beyond this the realm of neither perception nor non-perception, and from this he arrived at the cessation of sensation and idea.

And Ananda cried out to the great Anuruddha in an agony:

"O my Lord—O Anuruddha, the Blessed One is dead!"

And he, leaning above that Peace, said with calm:

"Nay, brother Ananda. He has entered that state where sensation and ideas have ceased to be."

And all veiled their faces.

And the mind of Him who has thus Attained retraced its way downward again and passing through all the stages entered into the fourth stage of deep meditation and passing out of this he immediately entered the Great Peace.

And at the moment of his expiring the thunders of

Heaven broke forth roaring about them and there was a loud and terrible trembling of the earth and the voice of Him who is the First uttered this:

"All beings in the world must lose their compound selves and individuality, and even such a Master as this, he, unrivalled and endued with all the powers, even he has passed into the Nirvana."

And the voice of Indra, King of Gods, took up the tale.

"Transient are all component things.
They being born must die, and being
dead are glad to be at rest."

And Anuruddha the Great said these words:

"When he, the Desireless, lay in peace, so ending his span of life, resolute and with unshaken mind did he endure the pains of death, attaining his final deliverance from the Fetters."

But Ananda cried aloud:

"Then there was terror, then the hair rose on the head, when he who possessed all grace—the supreme Buddha died."

Thus spoke the Four Loves, from the highest to the lowest,—and these of the brethren who were not yet enfranchised from the passions wept and wailed in anguish, crying aloud:

"Too soon has the Blessed One died. Too soon has the Happy One departed. Too soon is the World's Light darkened."

But the great Arhats bore their sorrow calm and self-possessed, saying:

"Transient are all earthly things. How is it possible they should not be dissolved?"

And all that night did the great Sariputta and Anuruddha spend in high discourse, but Ananda wept nor could be comforted.

And in the morning the great Anuruddha addressed the sorrowing Assembly.

"Enough, my brethren. Weep not nor lament. Has not the Blessed One declared to us that it is in the very nature of things near and dear to us that we and they must part? How then can it be possible that anything born and thus containing within itself the necessity of dissolution should not dissolve? Weep no more. Even the spirits would reproach us. For they who have attained wisdom say, "Transient indeed are all component things. How is it possible they should not be dispersed? This cannot be."

And calling to Ananda he sent him into the town of Kusinara that he might tell the faithful Mallas that their Lord was departed and that in their true hands should be the burning.

And they came out lamenting, having made great and costly preparation, and they encased the body of the Lord in new cloth and folded sheets of wool and lastly in a vessel of iron for the burning, and having clad themselves in new garments eight chieftains of the Mallas lifted the body, and they bore it through their little town to their own shrine, and there in the presence of the Order with devotion and spices and flowers and perfumes they did what was needful, and the body of the Lord passed into gray ash, fulfilling all even to the uttermost.

"Bow down with clasped hands.

Hard, hard is it to meet with a Buddha through hundreds of ages."

But they knew in whose presence they had stood.

This also have I heard.

The great Ananda, casting aside the fetters of love and retaining only its radiance, became a mighty Arhat and laid aside all sorrow.

After these things, one day it so chanced that one of

the brothers sat with Pingiya the aged Brahman, the disciple of the Lord, and Pingiya from the fullness of his heart spoke of the Blessed One, saying:

"As he saw the Way, so he taught it, he, the very wise, the passionless, the desireless Lord, and how should he do otherwise, for in him was no shadow nor turning of untruth. I will praise the voice of him who was without folly, who had left arrogance far behind. It is he only, the Dispeller of darkness, the high Deliverer, who giveth light."

And seeing his love, the other said:

"How then can you stay away from him even one instant, O Pingiya?"

And the old man replied:

"Not even for one instant do I stay away from him, my brother. Vigilant day and night I see him in my mind. In reverencing him do I spend the night, and verily I think I am not far from him."

And he mused awhile and added this:

"I am worn out and feeble, but my heart, venerable brother, is joined to him for ever."

And lo, as Pingiya sat and said this word, there shone about them a great light and Pingiya beheld the Blessed One stand there in majesty that cannot be uttered. And he said these words:

"Strong is thy faith, O Pingiya, and it shall be made glad. Fear not. You too shall reach that further shore, the haven of the realm of death."

## CHAPTER XXII

AND when the burning was done, the faithful Mallas gathered the bones and they took them to their Council Hall and surrounded them with a lattice-work of spears and a rampart of bows, and there for seven days they did them reverence and homage with solemn dance and music and garlands and perfumes.

And the King of Maghada sent to beg a portion of the relics, for he said: " The Blessed One was of the soldier caste and so too am I; I am worthy to receive a portion and I will set over it a sacred monument and hold a solemn feast."

And other peoples, and among them the Sakyas of Kapila,—the Lord's own people—sent demanding each a portion. And the Sakyas said:

" He who has thus Attained was the pride of our race. We are worthy to receive a portion, and we will put up a sacred monument and celebrate a solemn feast."

And so it was with six more peoples all demanding their portion, and the true Mallas grew angry, for they loved the Lord, and they replied:

" The Blessed One died in our land and he is ours. We will not give away any of the relics."

But the wise Brahman Dona rose amongst them and said this:

" Hear, sirs, one word from me. Our Lord taught forbearance, and gentleness was the law of his lips. Would it not be unseemly that strife should arise over the relics of him who was in all things highest? Sirs, let us all with one accord unite in friendly harmony to divide these precious relics into eight portions."

And they asked him, this being so, to undertake the division, and he answered " Be it so," and with scrupulous care he divided the relics, asking for himself the vessel that he might set a monument over it.

And to the Moriya people (who too late asked their share of the precious relics), seeing their grief they gave the embers of the pyre, and these with all reverence they took away.

Thus is the story told of Him who cast aside earthly love and riches and power that he might open the way to the myriads of mankind who have trodden it after him and who will tread it until all things merge in the unity and reconcilement of the Peace. For like a bright shining went forth the words of the Lord unto the ends of the earth, and those countries that have not heard shall yet hear and rejoice, for in Him were all wisdom and all love. And Kings and Emperors have heard and adored, and peasants looked up in gladness to see the night of sorrow dawn into the sunrise of joy.

And for that man who desires no longer the illusions of earth, ended—ended is the passing from death to death, the illusion of that false self and ego being slain over whom alone death has dominion! For the All in whom we are One is life and not death.

Yet do not think that all the appearances of this world are wholly illusion for that was not the Teaching of the Lord. No; but he taught that the five senses cannot see nor hear nor touch nor the dissolving brain apprehend Absolute Truth, and that this being so there is only relative truth for those unenlightened who see but as in a glass darkly, while those who have attained enlightenment, as did He who has thus Attained, behold the Truth face to face.

Therefore here we see things but as they can appear

to us and not in their true Being, and are most mistaken and deceived.

Furthermore it is a strange thing and not to be uttered in words how by following the narrow way of right thinking and right doing is the cleansed perception attained. But the Lord said: "Do thus and thus, and you shall know." And so it is.

And to the weak and poor in spirit as to the great of mind he did not say:

"Believe this, for so it is told you," but "Do this, and little by little, as when a man climbs a mountain the earth unfolds beneath him, for yourselves you shall see and know, needing no testimony from another—No, not even from the ancient scriptures, the Vedas, the Vedanta or any Brahman nor another. For the Kingdom of Heaven is within you. Look inward and see it and be glad." Thus the Lord taught and so it was.

And because this is so I who have seen many teachings of the old writings and of the Brahmans pass away in later knowledge have never seen one jot or one tittle of the Law pass rebuked into oblivion, neither shall I, nor any other. Knowledge is a good thing and a great, but all knowledge that comes through the brain and the five senses shall be rebuked later or sooner by the majesty of the Truth and shall crumble and pass. Only he who perceives beyond knowledge and sees beyond sight can apprehend these matters and so sit above error, being one with the One, and beyond that is the Nirvana, and even beyond the Nirvana it may well be there are states inconceivable in glory.

As for the ignorant, nothing is as they think it and they move through a world of distorted forms most alien to the Truth, just as in the lower consciousness of insect, reptile, and beast the forms perceived by them are still more alien from the Truth, for consciousness evolves from lowly beginnings. And this must be so since the thing seen is shaped by him who sees it through his own fettered consciousness, the limits of which he can in no way escape until he reaches that perception to which the perception of the ignorant is as the snail's or worm's to the man's, becoming thus a part of the Universal Consciousness.

Yet let us not think that Reality is far from us. It lies about and in us and we walk in it and see it not, and in the higher perception bright things move about us and we of the lower perception see them no more than the blind man the sunshine in which he sits, and they touch us with strange instincts and visitings through the dark and we do not know, and our heart calls them to come nearer and there is silence.

So, for those who have eyes to see and ears to hear, the Blessed One summed up all teachings of the wise men of old and those who are yet to come, and no more can be added to it though it shall be more clearly understood as time and knowledge join hands. Therefore walk in the Way.

And whereas there are wise men of the West who teach that there is but one life in this world of form and illusion, one hope of development and knowledge,—I say this: Very wise and near the Truth must be those men of the West if one life of twenty, thirty, ninety years suffices to free them from the fetters of ignorance and render them perfect as their Father in Heaven (for so they phrase it) is perfect. With us this is not so, nor yet do we hold that any of the Buddhas can pay the debt of another nor lift his sins from his shoulders, holding that the debt incurred must be paid by the debtor, and this for the sake of immortal Justice and for his own sake also. For the Law is evolution in the innermost as in the mortal body. First the lowly beginning, the seed in black earth. Then the tender shoot, the waxing strength of trunk and bough till they can bear the glory of expanding blossom, and last, the perfect fruit. And in one life this cannot be. And so have all the Buddhas taught.

Yet another thing. It was said by our Wisest that the man who truly perceives sits above good and evil and may do what he will. Is this a hard saying? How can it be?

It is because the Truth is now his will. It is his being; he sits in it and it in him, and the Truth and he are one. How should such a man think; "This is right. I will do it. This is evil; I will not do it," any more than he will think; "I must breathe or I shall die," considering each breath or heart-beat? How can sin draw him any more than the writhing of the snake tempts to imitation the man who walks erect? These things are the necessary laws of the beginner in the Way. They are stages of the Noble Eightfold Path, but for the Enlightened, they who see things as they are, laws have no meaning, for they themselves are Law.

And this is the faith that must triumph, for Wisdom is its sceptre and Knowledge its footstool, and the science of the schools its slave to follow where it has led the way.

Did not the Blessed One say—"We know. He who has thus Attained has nothing to do with theories."

And great is the patience of the Law, for Eternity is its own and of time it knows nothing.

And now in ending I write down a few maxims which the wise have made for those who did not see the Face nor hear the Voice of Him who has thus Attained, that they also may consider and attain. For these are steps on the Way. "Let a man learn to comprehend the True Nature of the World of Law. Then will he perceive that all things are but the production of Mind."

"In all living creatures there exists and has existed from the beginning the nature of the Law. All, by this nature, contain the original essence of Enlightenment. Wherefore birth and death and even the Nirvana itself are transcended and become for us a dream of the night that is gone, being lost in a greater Light."

"To the eye of flesh, plants and trees appear to be gross matter. But to the eye of the Buddha they are composed of minute spiritual particles."

"Grass, trees, countries, the earth itself, all these shall wholly enter into Enlightenment."

"Hail to the Buddhas of the Three Worlds, who are all but One in the One Mind."

So I end.

With lips of clay have I told that which cannot be uttered and with mortal thought have I set forth the Highest. And well I knew this could not be, for it is above the flesh and the tongue cannot speak it.

Glory to the Blessed One, the Holy, the Perfect in Enlightenment!

COLLINS' NEW 7/6 FICTION

# HELEN NICHOLSON

## THE THREE FACES

### *A Romance of Southern Spain*

THE scene of this romantic and dramatically unfolded episode is laid near Granada, in the wild and beautiful mountains of Southern Spain. From the moment that Godet is drawn into his adventure, at the Inn of the Three Faces, we are led swiftly and with the inevitability of Fate to the solving of the mystery of the Cortijo del Aire. How Godet read the meaning of the Three Faces and helped the two young lovers, whose story is intertwined with his own, and how he finally triumphed over don Luis, his powerful and subtle adversary, whose personality broods like a shadow over the book, are all matters of absorbing interest. The story is pervaded by the inimitable humour of the Spanish peasants, and the marvellous colour and atmosphere of these Alpujarra mountains. In the end it is Inocencia, the mountain girl, who with her lantern, guides Godet to the happiness and freedom he has always sought.